Unpacking

A Memoir

By Hollywood Script Consultant

Dr. Linda Seger

Praise for Linda Seger's *Unpacking*

Here's what's wonderful about Linda Seger's new book *Unpacking*...

For those of you lucky enough to have experienced Linda's enthralling lectures, her transformative script coaching, or her many best sellers, it will come as no surprise that she's a terrific writer and storyteller, or that *Unpacking* is fun, inspiring, and emotionally powerful.

But her memoir touched me even more deeply than that—because I've had the great fortune of knowing Linda for more than forty years, and I got to share the stage with her in many places near and far, as we each shared our own approach to screenwriting and storytelling.

So as I began reading *Unpacking* and experiencing the many exciting, challenging, victorious, and impactful moments of her life, I got to see *how* the qualities I've long admired (and envied!) in Linda came to be—her brilliance, wisdom, clarity, generosity, openness, determination, and especially her *courage*.

From her mother, who saw a world of endless possibility even in their small-town existence, to the stream of teachers who nurtured Linda's love of theater, psychology, spirituality, and humanity, to her friends and loved ones around the world—they all had a part in her never-ending thirst to experience whatever life offered, always growing and questioning and challenging herself to be the best person she could be.

At first I thought the title *Unpacking* referred only to the countless trips she's made to every corner of the world. But now I realize that this book is far more than that. It's a gift from someone we treasure who has reached the end of her career, and is sharing with us the lessons, friendships, wisdom, joy, inspiration, and love she has collected over a lifetime.

So be moved and inspired by this book, as I was. It will serve you—and the stories you tell—wherever your own journey takes you.

—Michael Hauge, Script and Story Consultant/
Author: *Writing Screenplays That Sell; Selling Your Story in 60 Seconds; Storytelling Made Easy*

Linda Seger has indeed had an outstanding life and career. She has influenced thousands of people directly through her many best-selling books and world-wide seminars, as well as through individual consultations on people's scripts—all of which have contributed to much better stories on so many levels.

Each chapter in Linda's memoir includes a section on UNPACKING, where lessons learned from that specific era, events, or focus are analyzed and presented as wise nuggets the rest of us can use.

If you like to do 'armchair traveling' this is also a good read for that. Linda's wall map with pins on all the places she's traveled is well-described in the pages of her memoir *Unpacking*. Her adventures have definitely added to my "Travel To-Do" list.

Linda was a generous mentor to me when I first began my own story-consulting business. Her enthusiastic support and the many connections she made for me led to some of my best experiences, including prestigious organizations, trips abroad, and long-term clients.

With a mixture of wonder, curiosity, inventiveness, generosity, respectfulness, and fun, Linda's encounters with the world, with individuals, and with stories are always rich and engaging. Read *Unpacking* and learn; read it and be inspired; read it and enjoy.

—Pamela Jaye Smith, Mythologist/Author/
Intl. Consultant and speaker/
Award-winning Writer-Producer-Director

Dr. Linda Seger is a force of nature. There are many ways to be pulled into her vortex of influence. You could read one of her best-selling books on screenwriting or religion and spirituality, you could attend one of her powerful seminars, or you could be in her presence working on a project. Her primaeval energy will transform you as she guides you to your greatest work. Her memoir spells out the genesis, chapter and verse, and culmination of the evolutionary force called Linda Seger. We all have stories that we live and tell. This is Linda's incredible story through the winding road of childhood, theology, acting, and directing, as a famous writer, captivating lecturer, world traveler, horsewoman, pianist, and wife. Read and allow it to inspire you.

—John Winston Rainey, Screenwriter/Author/Script Consultant

Unpacking is a collection of compelling stories of making "a good girl great!"

With unflinching candor and increasing perception, Linda shares challenges and hard-won personal and professional truths achieved on her journey from a small town in Wisconsin to making her mark all over the globe as a Hollywood insider and script consultant.

Linda is generous, funny, and self-deprecating, as she reveals dynamic relationships with her husband, friends, collaborators, teachers, and students. Her many self-revelations along the way lead not only to professional and material success, but also to a robust and shining spiritual success. Linda is always relatable, and we celebrate her evolution!

—Susan Baldwin Stroh, Memoir Workshop Leader/Collaborative Writer on Eighteen Published Memoirs/Memoir Author

Linda Seger is special. This book reveals some of what she has accomplished, some of what is behind the scenes, and some of a person who lives and learns through the ups and downs of life and the many manifestations of love.

—Reverend Patrick Hurley

Unpacking is the best possible title for this open-hearted memoir by Linda Seger. How do the varied and wide-ranging elements of a life that encompasses a spiritual degree, performances as both a piano diva and an equestrienne, international seminars, and a series of industry-defining books fit into her suitcase?

In this open-hearted memoir, Linda reveals her strengths and foibles with enviable honesty. And she delivers an ongoing feast of lived experience not as a chronology, but thematically, having come to understand the arc and structure of her own life with the same razor-sharp insights that made her the founder of the script-consulting industry and its most enduringly successful practitioner.

—Mara Purl, Best-selling Author of the Milford-Haven Novels

Also by Linda Seger

Screenwriting Books/Film Books

Making a Good Script Great:
A Guide to Writing and Rewriting

Creating Unforgettable Characters:
A practical guide to character development in films,
TV series, advertisements, novels, & short stories

The Art of Adaptation:
Turning Fact and Fiction into Film

The Collaborative Art of Filmmaking:
From Script to Screen
(Co-Written with Edward J. Whetmore)

Making a Good Writer Great:
A Creativity Workbook for Screenwriters

When Women Call the Shots:
The Developing Power and Influence of Women in
Television and Film

Advanced Screenwriting:
Taking Your Writing to the Academy Award Level

Writing Subtext:
What Lies Beneath

And the Best Screen Play Goes to . . .
Learning from the Winners

You Talkin' to Me?:
How to Write Great Dialogue
(Co-Written with John Winston Rainey)

Spirituality Books by Linda Seger

*Beyond Linear Thinking:
Changing the Way We Live and Work*
(Previously published as *Web Thinking*)

*God's Part in Our Art:
Making Friends with the Creative Spirit*

What Our Mamas Taught Us

Reflections With God While Waiting to Be Healed

The Alphabet Prayer
(Co-Written with Peter Hazen Le Var)

*Spiritual Steps on the Road to Success:
Gaining the Goal Without Losing Your Soul*

*Seeking The Light:
A Quaker Journey for Quakers and Non-Quakers*

*Jesus Rode a Donkey:
Why Millions of Christians Are Democrats*

Unpacking: A Memoir

Copyright © 2025 by Dr. Linda Seger

Softcover ISBN: 978-1-7377982-7-9

Published in the United States by Red Typewriter Press, P.O. Box 535, Cascade, CO 80809.

Cover design by Nick Zelinger: http://nzgraphics.com.

Interior design by Carmen Barber: KeepingYouWriting@gmail.com.

Scripture quotations marked KJV are taken from the Holy Bible, King James Version.

All rights reserved. No part of this book may be reproduced or transmitted in any form or by any means, electronic or mechanical, including photocopying, recording, or by any information storage and retrieval system, without permission in writing from the copyright owner.

Table of Contents

Foreword xvii
Preface xxi
Acknowledgments xxv

Part One:
The Foundations of My Life

Chapter One
    My Supporting Character 29

Chapter Two
    **The Most Magnificent Woman
    I Ever Met—My Mom** 39

Chapter Three
    My Friend Mandy 57

Chapter Four
    My Love of Drama 69

Chapter Five
    Dr. Wayne Rood 83

Part Two:
My Brilliant Career

Chapter Six
    **Starting My Life
    in the Film Biz** 95

Chapter Seven
    **My Brilliant Career Consultant
    Judith Claire** 111

Chapter Eight
**The Perks of
Teaching Seminars** 133

Chapter Nine
**Let Me Not Be Crazy
About Money** 171

Chapter Ten
**Famous People I Met or
Was in the Presence Of** 183

Chapter Eleven
**Famous People Who Said
Bad Things About Me** 199

Chapter Twelve
**My Magnificent Chapter—
The Horses** 211

Part Three:
Crisis Points

Chapter Thirteen
**But How Do I Get
Off the Mountain?** 225

Chapter Fourteen
**Saving a Life Isn't All It's
Cracked Up to Be** 239

Chapter Fifteen
Crisis in Bulgaria 259

Chapter Sixteen
Medical Crises 279

Part Four:
Transformations

Chapter Seventeen
Of Boys and Men 295

Chapter Eighteen
My Dear Peter 315

Chapter Nineteen
Spiritual Transformations 337

Chapter Twenty
Singing in Carnegie Hall 363

Chapter Twenty-One
Trying to Do Better................... 379

Chapter Twenty-Two
Unpacking the Present 399

About the Author.......................... 409

Dedicated to my dear husband
Peter Hazen Le Var

Foreword

I was honored when Linda asked me to write a foreword to her memoir. My big claim to fame is that I knew her back when, before she was Linda Seger Script Consultant. Aside from her hometown Peshtigonians, I may be her oldest known associate. We were both Cherubs at Northwestern University—a National High School Institute program for high school drama students. I still have a mimeographed program for the play she worked on as a stage manager. Cut to a couple decades later at a party when her husband, Peter, recognized the connection to Northwestern, and Linda and I reunited on this very special and common ground.

I can say, not in hindsight because I knew it while it was happening, that Linda was different from most of the rest of us. Adjectives come easily. Remarkable, extraordinary, determined, saintly, grounded in faith, self-aware. You will see for yourself in these pages. What Linda sets out to do, she does with single-minded commitment and hard work. She marks a path to success, and she gets on that path and does not waver—despite setbacks or obstacles, even as severe as physical disabilities (and even that she took on with the military precision of a dutiful soldier). Whatever she does, she goes all in.

Many threads run through Linda's life, but I think the fabric itself is humility. I don't mean the humility of admitting a mistake or being a shrinking violet (she is not). I mean the humility to admit one is lacking knowledge or expertise, and not being too proud to seek out those with the information and skill. You will see in these pages words like "teacher," "instructor," "specialist," "advisor," many, many times. Linda's passion and respect for proper learning is exceptional—she is a dedicated learner.

I got my first glimpse of this when she walked in one day in this smashing chic outfit with a very snazzy belt. She had hired a fashion consultant, and she beamed as she told us all about it. This was long before in-store fashion consulting was a thing. She wanted to dress more professionally, and she confessed that she didn't have a clue how to do it. The rest of us just read Vogue . . . and dreamed. (She was also the first person I knew to lease a car—before anyone else was doing it. The car was red.) That was Linda, admit you need help and get the help you need; don't be an arrogant fool who thinks they can wing it. You will see as you read this memoir that this was and is a constant in Linda's life—and is a valuable habit for all of us to consider.

I told Linda she should call her book "The Girl from Peshtigo," but she said *no*, she had settled on "Unpacking." So I'll call this foreword The Girl from Peshtigo, because she is and will always be that 'small-town girl' who lives with the kind of integrity and guilelessness we associate with the expression. And, someone who responds with awe and gratitude. She has traveled the world, and never become jaded. In fact, only twice did I even know her to complain—

once when the promised accommodations were misrepresented, and once when a host derailed her evening plans. Into the unknowns she ventured with a tolerance and trusting spirit that I again chalk up to a kind of humility. Take it as it lays. Carry on. The ultimate definition of adventurous—and faith.

So enjoy this memoir, and see what insights might inspire your own life. That is what will make Linda the happiest—seeing what she can do to make things better for you. That was the mantra of her consulting business and of her books, including this one.

In closing, if you have followed her on social media or noticed any photos of her, you will see that she is always smiling, always. A genuine, joyful smile—not for the camera, but for life itself. A life she has lived . . . going all in.

> ~ Lindsay Smith, Screenwriter/Artist
> www.lindsaysmithart.com

Preface

I have always loved stories. I love how they take us to different lands and introduce us to characters—some who our parents would not want us to meet and others who would make the best of friends. I love what they tell us about the human condition and about who we are. They tell us about our possibilities of transformation, which can go toward the bad or the good. I love how stories deal with the themes in our lives—greed, jealousy, lust for what we shouldn't be yearning for, and the big themes of self-sacrifice and heroism and courage and the triumph of the human spirit.

When I was young I decided I wanted to be a writer, and I presumed I would write fiction. When I wrote my first book, *Making a Good Script Great*, in 1986, it was one of the most totally positive experiences in my life, and I realized that I wanted to write nonfiction, but I wanted to work with writers who wrote fiction. When I entered the film business, I did not want to be a screenwriter. I wasn't sure exactly what I wanted—because what I wanted to do didn't exist. The first time I consulted on a script, I felt triumphant. I had truly made a difference in this writer's life and in his approach to solving the script problems which he had been unable to see. I liked being the objective eye and the guide and the nurturer of this writer's talent. I loved the excitement that the writer felt when he had a new grasp on how to make his script better and was eager to go back into the difficult creative process.

When I consulted on the first script and then the second and the third and then many, I realized I had found my calling. In spite of all the difficulties of creating a business that didn't exist, marketing it, getting clients, learning the best process to get the best out of the writer—all of that was a joy to me and continued to be for my entire career from 1981 to 2020. I adored my career, and I adored the life that I managed to create.

I hope you enjoy this journey that includes complex relationships, challenging interactions, big adventures, and my search for insights and the underlying themes that made the journey so rich and meaningful.

~ Linda Seger

Acknowledgments

Thank you:

To my assistant Jenn Wagner who typed and stuck with for me for this whole book. I thank her for her reliability and commitment and good spirits.

To my editors Carmen Barber, Marjorie Vawter, and Teresa Crumpton.

To my cover designer Nick Zelinger.

To my readers who gave me feedback as I was writing these chapters: Lynn Lee, Peter Le Var, Cathleen Loeser, John Winston Rainey, Lynn Rosenberg, Jana Rutledge, Lindsay Smith, Pamela Jaye Smith, Liz Spier, and Susie Stroh and to Haley Woolf who gave me feedback on Chapter 21.

To Heidi Bailey who came to my rescue at the last step, when the internet went down in our neighborhood and I couldn't access the book.

And always to my dear husband Peter Hazen Le Var.

> Thank you all for your generosity and insights.

Part One:
The Foundations of My Life

Chapter One
My Supporting Character

I couldn't write this book without recognizing a supporting character that will travel throughout the chapters—my little hometown of Peshtigo, Wisconsin. When I grew up, there were 2,504 people living there—the last four being my father Linus, my mother Agnes, my sister Holly, and me.

What's Peshtigo Like?

If you look at the map of Wisconsin, you'll see that it looks like your left hand. The space between your thumb and your first finger is the Bay that forms part of Lake Michigan. If you veer off to the thumb and go north, that's Door County where the cherry blossoms and art colonies are. It's beautiful. The place where the thumb joins the hand is Green Bay, Wisconsin, where the Green Bay Packers come from.

If you drive fifty miles straight north from there, you'll be in Peshtigo. If you have little fingers, the tip of your fingers will be where Upper Peninsula Michigan is. We were just ten miles from Menominee, Michigan. If you look at your right hand, that's the state of Michigan. But that's not where I lived. I lived in Wisconsin.

Where is Peshtigo?

We are located at exactly the halfway point between the equator and the North Pole at 45° latitude. There's a marker outside of town that lets tourists know that if they stand there, in a very, very small way, they are at the center of the universe. My father owned the local drugstore and was the pharmacist and was much loved for his generosity, his good care, and his sweet disposition. My mother felt differently, especially as the years went on when she craved a more exciting life. She was a brilliant pianist and piano teacher and voice teacher. She was President of the PTA and President of the Women's Club. I used to quote the line from the movie *Julia* when Dashiell

Hammett recognized the drive that Lillian Hellman had and told her, "You should've been a mayor of a small town." My mother would've been a good one.

There are lots of lakes and trees and forests and beautiful leaves changing in the fall. And seemingly, to an adventurous little soul, nothing exciting ever happened. Well, except for the Great Peshtigo Forest Fire.

The Great Peshtigo Forest Fire

The worst forest fire in the history of the United States was the Peshtigo Forest Fire on October 8, 1871. In case that date rings a bell—it was the same day as the Great Chicago Fire, which was not nearly as bad. Our whole town of Peshtigo was wiped out, and the death toll was around 1200 people. The surviving population ran from the heat of the flames to the Peshtigo River and stayed the night there with the cows and the horses and the men and the women and the children.

Look up any list of the greatest forest fires in the history of the country, and Peshtigo keeps coming up as number one. That's my little town.

Other than that, there wasn't much excitement going on in the town, which had one business street which included my dad's drugstore, the butcher store, the shoe store, the furniture store, more bars than gas stations, and definitely more bars than the one Catholic Church and the four Protestant churches in town. Some of the greatest consumption of Wisconsin beer happened in this little town, most of it from Milwaukee. We hold some kind of record for beer drinking.

And Then There Was the Great Peshtigo Bank Robbery

There was one other exciting thing that happened in Peshtigo—the Great Peshtigo Bank Robbery of 1956. I was sitting in my fifth-grade class, undoubtedly once more thinking that nothing exciting ever happened in Peshtigo, when the news came to us that there had been a bank robbery, and the bank robbers were still on the loose. This was wonderfully exciting to a young girl craving adventure. It was the real thing, not just excitement from the books I'd read and my own personal daydreams. Somebody was shot (but not killed), and I wondered if I had caused this whole catastrophe because of my yearning for adventure.

Within five hours the whole scenario was figured out, and the bandits were captured. The robbers came to town intending to rob a small bank since it looked like it would be easy. They went to the Peshtigo State Bank, but there were so many people there giving and getting money it looked a little too dangerous. So they drove three blocks down to the Peshtigo National Bank, and they robbed it instead. They fired one shot which ricocheted off the counter and hit one of the tellers in the chin (she was okay after medical care). The robbers then took off in their getaway car—down the only dead-end road out of town. The strong arm of the law called in reinforcements from as far away as Oconto fifteen miles down the road. They then asked Mr. DeHart, the only person in town with a small airplane, to take his plane up and see if he could find where they had gone. He called back, "They're at the end of the dead-end road and are now in the swamp trying to get away." With sirens blaring, about eight cop cars congregated by the swamp, and the men had no choice but to take off their pants so the cops could see there were no guns in those pockets. Then with their conventional white shirts coming just down far enough to show off their young boyish legs and still be appropriate for the Peshtigo Times newspaper, they waited by the swamp with their hands up until they were taken away.

That was exciting—from 10 a.m. to 2 p.m.

If there was going to be excitement in Peshtigo, you either waited for eighty-five years or you created it yourself.

Mom and Dad Added to the Excitement

My parents were good at creating excitement. My mom helped put on the local variety show every summer. Lots of kids and their parents brought out hidden talents—they sang, danced, told jokes, or juggled. My dad was part of the Midnight Madness Sale, which happened every summer between 9 p.m. and midnight where people went shopping in their pajamas. It didn't matter whether there was anything you wanted to buy—you wanted to be part of the excitement!

For those years from late grade school through high school, my parents recognized how protective our town was and tried to give us experiences on vacations that would broaden us and bring us into the bigger world. When I was twelve, we went to Washington, DC, for a week, and we went to a dude ranch in Colorado for a week when I was thirteen. In high school there was the junior and senior play, which led me to turn my sights to The Theatre where exciting things were happening all the time—well, at least within the plays.

I yearned to get out and see the world, yet as the years went by—in college and after—I began to see how very precious this little town was, a place with more cows than people. In the summer there was the smell of fresh corn in the fields. There was the quietness of the river and the tranquility of Lake Michigan. Perhaps it's like getting a puppy when you're in grade school and watching it grow and it became so natural that you yearned for something much bigger. And then at some point as you watched your old beautiful mutt sleeping and snoring on the rug, you realized that this was part of the foundation of your life. It was something unique and special and beautiful, and you suddenly felt that sense of home and security and even love. Peshtigo set my values in place—midwestern small-town values of accepting others who were poor or rich. Working for what you wanted rather than feeling entitled. And a sense of contentment while still dreaming big dreams. These values gave me a vision of a horizon to explore. And it was fine to explore. Deep down, I'm a Midwesterner living in the West. I'm a small-town girl who eventually had a lot of good exciting adventures in my life.

Unpacking

There are two places I consider home—Peshtigo and Colorado. The dude ranch vacation introduced me to the West, the beautiful mountains, and the cowboy culture, which I had found in all of my favorite TV shows. Growing up I would straddle the back of our straight back armchair and use the venetian-blind cords as reins, pretending I was riding a horse. I would watch my favorite cowboy shows—*Cheyenne, The Cisco Kid, Roy Rogers and Dale Evans, The Lone Ranger,* and even *Lash LaRue*—the guy in black leather with a snappy whip.

The first time I entered the Colorado Rockies, it felt like a wonderous miracle. I turned around and looked out the back windows of the car, and we were suddenly surrounded by mountains on all sides. Every curve showed a new beauty. In the years following it was almost heartbreaking to me to think of Colorado and not be there. I was determined to get back, which I did when I went to college in Colorado Springs in 1963. Following college, I was determined to live there, which I have done since 2002. It is an everyday miracle to be in this beautiful land and to realize that Peshtigo made me.

Linda's Trivia

Favorite place in the world: My little town of Cascade, Colorado

Population: 1,243 (which includes the surrounding rural areas)

Altitude: 7,250 feet

Major businesses: Two restaurants, a rock store, a Subaru repair shop, and its own post office

Fun fact: When I moved to Cascade the young woman who lived immediately next door to me was reading my book *Making a Good Script Great*. She found this coincidence incredible, and so did I.

Chapter Two
The Most Magnificent Woman I Ever Met—My Mom

My mother recounted a sermon to me that asked the question: "How many people did it take to make you who you are?" I might add to this question, "How many events and experiences and decisions did it take to fine-tune your personality, your ethics, your relationships, your courage, and your kindness? If you removed one of these people or events from your life, would you still be the person you are today?"

Certainly, many people leave their sweet mark on us in one way or another. They influence us, give us a piece of advice that guides us through the years and leads us in a better direction. They add details to our lives. They add nuances. There are people who reach into our core and in one way or another, change that core for the better. We are embraced by what they contribute to us. It surrounds us. It penetrates into our very souls. These people help us actualize ourselves and fulfill ourselves and become more authentic human beings. We have no idea who we would be if these people had not been in our lives.

My Amazing Mother

My mother, Agnes Katherine Graebner Seger, was the most magnificent woman I ever met. My uncle said the same thing about Eleanor Roosevelt, whom he met many years ago. I have no trouble with this comparison.

Mom was what one might call a handsome woman. Kind of a big nose. Sort of big ears. A dark-olive complexion, crooked teeth with a smile that was not so much beautiful—like the Hollywood smile of women with really good teeth—but a smile that lit up her eyes and made them sparkle. It was a giving look. She was, in some ways, a typical 1950s housewife who wore house dresses, red lipstick, and rouge. She drove us to school every day and put a fur coat over her night gown for the drive. I was slightly embarrassed by this outfit and always hoped she wouldn't get stopped.

My mother was a visionary. She saw life in a big way. She had plans, and she saw possibilities. She made things happen, and I have no idea how she did it.

Agnes Katherine Graebner Seger was a beautiful pianist. It's very possible that if she had not lived in the 1950s, she could have been a concert pianist. She won an international piano contest when she was eighteen, playing a beautiful piece of music called "Caprice Viennois" by Fritz Kreisler.

I have never been able to figure out how she developed that talent and that skill level, because her father was a minister at a conservative Lutheran church (Missouri Synod for those of you who know Lutheranism), and they were poor.

Mother's mother was a very humble woman whose job it was to cook and bake and clean. Neither of her parents were visionaries. My grandfather, whom I adored, was called "difficult" by my mother.

And yet, somebody must have nurtured her talent and opened opportunities for her. I wondered if somebody in the church was a good piano teacher and if my mother used the piano at the church. Or if someone gave them a piano for their home. I do know my mother used to call old upright pianos "old clunkers," and my guess is that she played quite a few of those.

When I was born in 1945, I had a gracious and kind sister Holly who was a year and a half older than me. Our lives were filled with music. Mom had a number of piano students and would have little house concerts. Mother believed all of us had our little contributions to make. When I was four years old, and had not yet started lessons, I was the MC for one of these house recitals. I would sit next to the piano and then stand up and say, "Bonnie will play next," and then Bonnie would play, and then I would stand up again, perhaps after a little nod from my mother, and announce the next person—"Susie will play next."

Bonnie told me years later—since she was two years older than me—that I had a little watch and that when the other people would play, I would spend most of the time winding the watch before I announced the next number.

A Home Full of Music

Mom had piano students who floated in and out of our home. My sister and I also played piano, and it wasn't unusual for mom to sit down at the piano during the day and play pieces she had memorized.

Mom would often play the piano after dinner. When Holly and I were little, we would put on our fancy nightgowns and dance and sing in the living room to her music, pretending we were opera singers with hiccups. As we got a little older, we began to sing solos and then duets and then trios with Mom. Mom's theory on piano lessons was a belief that a good time to start a child on piano was age seven, but I begged for lessons, and I expect I started playing by age five or six.

As we got closer to late grade school and high school, mother would accompany all the kids who were entering the spring state music competition. She accompanied the cornet player, the flute player, and the trombone player, as well as accompanying the kids who sang solos and duets. She was the school choir accompanist as well.

I honestly don't remember any time when my mother was critical or judgmental of me at the piano—no matter how unskilled I was. Mother believed that a piano teacher should give a child a good musical experience. I grew up with encouragement and the joy of music.

Mom set up all sorts of musical experiences. When I was thirteen my mother was the President of the Women's Club of our little town of Peshtigo, and she decided it would be fun for five of us girls to sing "'Twas the Night Before Christmas" for the club's Christmas party. We got dressed up in our nightgowns and carried our stuffed animals. Mom taught us harmonies and each of us had a phrase to say by ourselves—my phrase being "His cheeks were like roses, his nose like a cherry!" No one was slighted. There was no competition. In fact, I don't even remember any nervousness. It was simply fun.

My Nurturing Mom

Mom was not afraid to think outside the box. She nurtured the smallest talent. She praised people. She helped people fulfill their talents and their gifts. Sometimes she saved others from dire consequences.

When we were adults, a family with two girls moved next door to my parents. The girls were about twenty years younger than my sister and me and came from a toxic family. Right before one of them was ready to go to college, their mother got so angry at her that she locked the girl in her room. The girl managed to call my mother and ask for help. Mom went to pick her up and arranged for her to live with them until it was time to go off to college.

My mother helped the older sister by encouraging her to become an exchange student in Australia, which had been beyond her sights, but not my mother's. This older sister also lived with my parents for a period of time. Mother recognized the girls were smart and that they needed help. The older sister eventually got a full scholarship to Yale and then a PhD at Oxford University. The younger sister got a full scholarship to Penn State and then an MA in Writing. She wrote her thesis on my mother and how that summer had changed her.

Mom had the ability to see what interested us. We wanted to explore—horseback riding, going out West, having more musical opportunities—and Mom would try to make them happen. It was never about material things we wanted, but about experiences.

Mom Loved New Experiences— for Her and Us

When I turned sixteen, I had a brunch for my birthday. Mother had to explain to me what a "brunch" was. One of my girlfriends told me years later, "I still remember that brunch. Nobody in Peshtigo had ever had a brunch. Your mom was always doing something special!"

She kept looking for opportunities for us, knowing that Peshtigo did not offer many. She didn't see us as becoming homemakers who never worked but people who found fulfilling things to do. Years later she told me, "I always wanted you to know that life was good."

Mom was never snobby or hoity-toity in any way. She made friends in this little town of 2,504—and she used every opportunity to contribute within the limits that were now part of her life. She stayed happy, although it was really tough for her when her two daughters went off to college and adulthood. Yet in her fifties Mom got cancer and survived, and when she was fifty-eight, she decided to go back for a master's degree at the University of Wisconsin in Milwaukee and changed her career from music to social work. She began to work outside the limits of Peshtigo, and began to re-create a life—knowing she couldn't really leave Peshtigo because my father was there. There was no talk of a divorce or any kind of separation. Instead, she began going to Tucson for about six weeks in the winter. Clearly my dad was not interested in traveling, and I certainly approved her choice of doing some things just for herself as long as he was taken care of, which he was.

Mom had no problem asking for exceptions when needed. I applied to Colorado College in the fall of my senior year and then applied to two other colleges in case I didn't get into CC. Colorado College wrote me back and asked if I was applying for Early Decision. "I guess so."

But there was a rub. For early-decision consideration, I was not supposed to have applied to other colleges but only to CC. I hadn't known that. Mom suggested that I write them and ask for an exception and tell them, "If you accept me, you will hear the cheers all the way from Peshtigo." The exception was made. I got in. We cheered. She always had my back.

When Mom went back to school, the teachers did not want to let an older student in, so she asked to see the head guy. He asked her, "Why would I let you in instead of somebody who is younger and has their whole career ahead of them?"

Mom answered, "I don't have the slightest idea!"

He laughed and said, "You're in!"

I was so proud of her. It was a tough two years, but she did it! And she became a role model for me when I went back for another MA degree when I was in my fifties.

The Downside of Love

My mother adored us and loved us. But there was an unusual downside to this wonderful love. Holly once said, "It can get to be a bit much." I understood what she was talking about. On the one hand Mother's love was not judgmental. She was not picky or belittling or critical. She guided us, and we followed quite willingly. We didn't feel controlled. On the other hand, she was a strong, domineering person. Her comments were the law, and it just took one look and a phrase for us to understand what we were and were not supposed to do.

When I was in college, I transferred to Western Reserve University for my junior year and was very unhappy. I wanted to return to Colorado College where I had spent my freshman and sophomore year, but Colorado didn't like to take re-transfers and said *no*. I mentioned to Mom I might take a semester off, and she gave me "that look" which told me clearly this was not an option. Since I had such a close relationship with Mom, the look of reproach was accepted. As it turned out, someone dropped out of Colorado College four days before school started and the college gave me her space so I could return and graduate from there.

Most of the time domineering people are negative and they try to force you into an identity that might not be who you really are. Mom was dominating in a positive way because she opened up opportunities and truly wanted the best for us. But the "best" for Mom might not have always been the best for us, even though it was wonderful in its own way. I eagerly fell into being so close to my mother that when I was in my twenties, I felt like I was my mother.

I needed to disconnect and be my own person. It can sometimes be more difficult to disconnect from love than to disconnect from non-love.

I began to disconnect by making decisions without telling my parents until after I had made them. When I was miserable in my first marriage, I decided to get a divorce. I informed my parents after I told my husband. I decided to go to seminary and applied and then told my parents about my decision.

I entered seminary when I was twenty-six years old and decided to study religion and the arts. I was determined to make it on my own and not ask for money from my parents. I felt there were strings attached when Mom sent a check, even when those strings were simply expecting a thank-you note. I was so determined not to get tangled up in any strings that I thought a thank-you note would do just that. It makes little sense to me now, but I returned the checks which I believe hurt her deeply.

I started seeing a therapist to help me get my head on straight—about my mother and about everything else in my life. I was clearly having an identity crisis and to some extent took it out on Mom. I'd have an insight in therapy and then would write letters where I criticized my mother for something she had done. My mother, being creative and big hearted, would write me back and say, "I had to put your letter in the freezer for three days to cool it off." This made me chuckle, and I realized I was being quite hard on her. I know at one point when I was at home, I brought her to tears. Thankfully my therapist was good, and Mom and I got through this rough patch.

If there was one consistent criticism she had of me, it was about my hair style. I had fine hair and big ears, and I was never able to get a hairstyle that looked good on me. My mother would sometimes make little picky remarks which frustrated me because I couldn't figure out how to find a great hairstylist.

Shortly before Mom died, she broke her hip and went into rehabilitation. When her rehabilitation was finished, I helped move her back to her assisted-living facility in

Tucson. I'd left Los Angeles quickly, and my hair was an absolute wreck. It was oily and stringy and needed washing and a good haircut. When I arrived she was not talking, but as I was ready to leave, she beckoned to me. She said the only words she spoke in those two days. Her sentence began with "your hair." I thought she was going to make a well-deserved comment. I came closer to her, and she started the sentence again. "Your hair is adorable." These were the last words she said to me. She died the following Monday. Those words made up for the lifetime of these few little criticisms when she picked at me, and of course I forgave her for everything immediately.

Unpacking

Mom taught me to be generous to others. To not be afraid to go after things that I wanted. To not be afraid to dream big. To keep a positive attitude. To not be afraid to be different—since Mom was clearly different from many of the people in our little town. Yet she fit in and found a way to contribute to our community of Peshtigo by including so many different people in her joyful experiences. She taught me to negotiate difficult situations and how to deal with difficult people so I could keep my own sense of self without having to argue and have a big blowup with others. We were not a family that did blowups, but I don't think we were a family that stuffed it either. I thought the communication channels were open, and Mother taught me to be able to analyze a situation and then figure out what to do about it. When I made big decisions—such as leaving my first husband and going to seminary—I always felt she had my back.

When I was in danger of losing the good positive attitude my mother had taught me—during my first marriage and during some tough days in graduate school—I would think about all Mother had done to instill these values in me. I became very intentional about protecting them. It became imperative that I not lose The Good Within, much of it instilled by Mom through her enduring love.

Linda's Trivia

My favorite human quality is generosity to others.

Chapter Three
My Friend Mandy

Mandy (not her real name) became my best friend during my senior year at Colorado College. She changed my life. She opened up new ways of thinking and reflecting and listening and being. She introduced me to a very profound and soulful way of being friends that prepared me for many more friendships in my life.

Mandy listened with her eyes. She listened to answers, read the face to see what else was going on, and asked follow-up questions—often deep and profoundly personal questions, which was not the Seger way of doing things. The Segers analyzed. Discussed. Shared. Assessed. Sometimes chattered and blubbered. And as my mother once said when my sister had complained that I had been talking for three hours straight, "Linda has something to say."

Meeting Mandy

We met in ballet class when I was a sophomore and she was a freshman. She knew all the ballet moves and had been dancing for many, many years. Me? Well, I probably didn't belong in that intermediate class. I had taken ballet when I was ten, and I took private ballet lessons when I was a senior in high school. The teacher of the college class didn't know what to do with me. I was not a beginner, nor was I good enough to be an intermediate. So, he suggested I take one beginning class a week and one intermediate class. There was no advanced class but even so, it was a stretch to put me in the intermediate class, and I was way out of my league.

Mandy was not. When Mandy did a grand jeté, leaping through the air, she seemed to float and just stay there and then gently came down. When I did one, it was almost like a little hop and a thunk.

We chatted occasionally after class, and one time went to a movie but did not become friends until I was a senior.

I decided to do some spiritual seeking my senior year because I felt I had inherited my religion from my parents and I needed to make it personal.

I knew that Mandy went to church, so I asked her if I could go to church with her. I thought she was going to the Unitarian church, but at this point she was going to the Bible church. It didn't matter to me where I stared this exploration. Mandy became the major influence at the beginning of my religious seeking.

Mandy's Impact on My Spiritual Seeking

Mandy and I began to read the Bible and had prayer time before dinner. She introduced me to other religious groups. She shared resources and the names of books I might be interested in reading. She didn't put pressure on me to do anything or go anywhere, but it was a very rich sharing time with her. And I began to get answers—about praying and feeling a connection with God and about the richness I found in the Bible.

Nurturing Our Friendship

My spiritual seeking became the foundation and the beginning point of our friendship. She also became a kind of Transformational Character for me over the years because she was a friend who could follow my journey, and I could follow hers. And for many years we tried to see each other once a year and then eventually every four or five years. Each time we met we asked each other: "How have I changed since last you saw me?" And we did notice changes. I remember one time when I was in seminary, Mandy told me I had become "quite eloquent." As we moved into our thirties and even forties, I mentioned that Mandy's sense of humor had come to the forefront and that we laughed more. A few times we did trips together. When I got my first royalty check in 1989, we met in New York, and I paid her expenses so we could see New York—the Statue of Liberty, Tea at the Plaza, a Broadway play, and a walk in Central Park.

The Strength of Our Friendship

As we got older, I realized the strength of our friendship was partly because we had such different paths and had insight into what it was like to be so different from each other. She was an introvert. I was an extrovert. She was very good at sitting in silence, lighting a candle, and just staring at it. I was very good at talking and doing things. I was career oriented and she had little interest in a career.

She went to graduate school to study psychology but quit after a short time. During that year I was married and miserable. Mandy and I talked at times on the phone about my misery. And when I was in my deepest despair, I realized that Mandy had always been very good at listening and asking me questions and leading me to reflection and my own personal insights. Perhaps it would be very helpful for me to be able to see her. I called and asked if I could come to Arizona and see her, and she asked, "When?"

I replied, "Tomorrow."

After a brief pause, she asked, "Could you come the day after tomorrow?"

I told her "Yes" and let my husband, Mike (not his real name), know I was going to be gone for a week.

Mandy Saves Me from My Miserable Marriage

When I got off the plane in Arizona, Mandy told me I was like a "caged bird that was suddenly free." She gave me a book by Abraham Maslow that had a lot to do with what it meant to be authentic and about value systems. We discussed the book. She asked me interesting questions such as, "If you were an ice cream, what flavor would you be?"

I told her, "Mint chocolate chip."

Then she asked, "What flavor would Mike be?"

"Pumpkin," I said.

She asked, "How do you feel about pumpkin?"

I told her I wasn't very fond of pumpkin.

Just talking to her led me to the conclusion that I had to leave. This was not because I disliked pumpkin. That would not hold up in divorce court. He belittled me, demeaned me, picked at me, and tried to control me.

Starting a New Life with Mandy's Help

When I left Mike, I realized that I needed to find some way to start a new life and be happy after a year of misery. I asked Mandy, "If I were to move to Arizona, would you like to get an apartment together?" (She was still in graduate school and would be there for a while longer.) It was agreed we would room together. I felt that Mandy could help me get back on my feet and start a more authentic and happier life. I started writing to colleges and universities in the Phoenix area to see if jobs were available in teaching, and then purely on faith, packed up my car and drove from Wisconsin to Arizona. Just before I got there, I received a phone call from one of the colleges—a Southern Baptist college called Grand Canyon College—telling me that their drama teacher had just dropped out and asked if I was still interested. "Absolutely!" I arrived in Phoenix, and Mandy told me plans had changed for her also—she was getting married. Nevertheless, we got an apartment for several weeks, and then she left and I continued in Phoenix.

We continued with our different lives, sharing, meeting, talking, listening, and being enriched by each other for many years.

A Changing Friendship

It was only recently, as we got into our late sixties and seventies after such a long and deep friendship, that I began to realize that what we had with this soulful connection was no longer there and what we now had was simply history. And history was not enough for me. I realized that she had little interest in what I was doing in my life— continuing to write books and playing piano—and that she was not sharing her life with me. She had a granddaughter whom she clearly adored but never told me anything about her, never sent me pictures even though I'd asked several times. None of my efforts seemed to help. Then the Great Political Divide entered into our lives. I am a Christian Democrat and had written a book about this titled *Jesus Rode a Donkey: Why Millions of Christians Are Democrats*. Mandy was a Trump supporter, and it was clear we could not talk about this. There was little sharing going on, and our values seemed to diverge. We no longer cared about the same things. Even though it was clear that there was much to talk about, we were no longer sharing our lives. Perhaps it was time to let this relationship go. I wrote her a long letter of goodbye, wrote her name on a piece of paper, and burned it in my fireplace and thought about the richness that had been there and served both of us so beautifully for so many years.

The Relationship Changes Again

In spite of this goodbye letter, she wrote me twice, and I decided, after the second letter, to accept this limited engagement. I usually wrote back within a few weeks. She wrote back about every two to four months. The letters were mostly us catching up, although I've tried to put some emotional content into my letters to her. Gradually, she's begun to share more. She has asked me questions and asked me to ask her questions. I am now, at the age of seventy-nine, re-engaging and letting the mystery unfold by answering her infrequent letters.

Unpacking

I have learned to see the gem of this friendship from the period of my life from my twenties into my sixties. Much of this time was formative for me since I needed to expand both outside and inside of myself. Mandy was such an important person to help me go deeper within, to listen, to be quiet, and to develop my introspective side. Instead of regretting this loss of our depth, I've learned to value what we once had.

As I reflect on our lives, I feel there is so much that we could talk about and share, even now. Mandy taught me how to be a friend and stay as a friend as long as the friendship endures. She taught me to value friendships and to be aware that some friends truly invest in a friendship and others do not. The friends I have now bring many good qualities to me, and I have tried to accept limits as well as expansions. With some friends, there is the occasional gracious lunch. Other friends are there by my side, through thick and thin. They bring sweetness, insights, and wisdom to me, and perhaps I am able to appreciate these qualities because of Mandy. Neither of us seem willing to give up on this friendship, and it is now open-ended in terms of what it is and what it will become.

Linda's Trivia

Mandy's mark on my life was to change me from a talker to someone who has learned to listen.

Chapter Four
My Love of Drama

I was a terrible actor. But I loved drama. I loved stories and characters and make-believe and pretend.

In my little town, there were very few opportunities for doing any kind of dramatic activities, except for music and an occasional variety show. We had the junior play. I got cast, but I had one line: "Hello Suzie, is Mike in here?" In the senior class play, I was cast as the maid—a little part where my big moment was falling down. When I got into college, I tried out for every play and eventually got cast my sophomore year for walk-on parts in the play *Galileo*. I was four different walk-on characters. My mom said, "Don't bump into yourself walking in while you're walking out." I had one line in the play: "Who is that?"

In college we also did the musical *Kismet*, and I was a harem girl in the chorus. I stood around and sang alto. In my junior year in college, I got cast in the Greek play, *Hecuba*, and had one line: "Surely no man could be so callous or so hard of heart that he could hear this woman's heartbroken cry and not be touched." I'm not sure that there is any good way to say this line, but it was taken away from me, and the new actor didn't do much better than I did.

Attending a Five-Week Drama Program that Changed My Life

Between my junior and senior years in high school, I attended the National High School Institute at Northwestern University. We were called Cherubs, and it was a very special program where they took seventy-five drama students from all over the United States. I have no idea how I got in unless it was my brilliant reading of the line: "Hello, Susie, is Mike in here?" The other seventy-four people in my group had gone to high schools where they had acting classes and did three plays a year. At Northwestern I experienced five weeks of theater and loved it. We painted sets. We did Reader's Theater. We took acting classes. We did make-up for each other. And each of us was in a play. They had to cast everybody in a play! Oh, thank God!

I tried out for *Diary of Anne Frank* and for *Finian's Rainbow* and for all the other plays, and I was cast in two one-act plays—Ionesco's *The Leader* and Edward Albee's *The Sandbox*. In *The Leader* I was part of the crowd and said, in unison, with the rest of the crowd: "The Leader. Here comes the Leader." In *The Sandbox*, I played the musician who had zero lines and played the flute on the beach. It may have been that I was the only person in that whole institute who was a flute player, and they needed a flute player.

But those five weeks changed my life. My mother said, "Maybe this will get theater out of your system!" But it did the opposite. And that was fine with my family.

And yet—in spite of all evidence to the contrary—I continued to love drama but couldn't figure out where there might be a place for me. But then a few things changed.

Taking Opportunities

In my sophomore year at Colorado College, my class (class of '67) created a Theater Workshop where students would direct one-act plays and produce our own work. Besides the main stage productions that were directed by the head of the drama department at Colorado College, now there would be new opportunities. I discovered directing. With my analytical mind, some people skills, and my ability to organize, directing suited me better. I had a good visual sense. I had a good sense of rhythm and movement. I didn't mind telling people what to do. So I volunteered to direct, and I directed, of course, *The Leader* and *The Sandbox*.

My junior year I took a bit of a detour. I was trying to pull together a BA degree in English, Drama, and Education and I simply could not get that at Colorado College. At that time they had a Fine Arts degree, but they didn't have a theater degree, so I transferred to Western Reserve University in Cleveland. I took some good drama classes, but I didn't like Cleveland. I wasn't able to create the major I wanted and I longed for Colorado. I was miserable. I went to see the movie *The Unsinkable Molly Brown* which took place in Colorado, which motivated me to apply as a re-transfer back to Colorado College. I yearned to return, but CC had informed me they don't like to take re-transfers. I asked them to make an exception. I didn't hear a word from them for three months, and I began to accept the fact that I would need to return to Cleveland. Four days before college started, Colorado College called and said someone had dropped out and if I wanted the space, I could have it. Absolutely! I was on the next train to Colorado.

Finding a Teacher Who Actually Appreciates Me

During my senior year, the Theater Workshop decided to do a three-act play and asked who might be interested in directing. I volunteered. I directed *Winterset* by Maxwell Anderson. I had Christmas vacation to prepare, and we then had ten days to put on a play.

During Christmas another little miracle happened. When I was in high school in Peshtigo, there was a high school in the neighboring city of Marinette, Wisconsin, that had a tremendous drama program. They did three plays a year, and I occasionally went to those plays. Harold Zahorik was the head of this program. I had not met him, but my mother knew about him, and she arranged for us to meet that Christmas. He helped me analyze and prepare to direct. He discussed how to approach the difficult scenes. He helped me interpret it and understand the background of it. He was an incredibly kind and supportive person—I finally found a drama teacher that seemed to "get" me.

When I got back to Colorado College, I was ready to go. There was a special bonus because the actor who had been the lead in many plays and was drop-dead gorgeous tried out for my play. Of course he was cast by me as the lead in this one. But I kept my eye on the ball. For ten days we worked all day long—and the play went on.

Another Opportunity Opens

Another opportunity opened my senior year of college. The one drama teacher at the college was not fond of me. This wasn't just because I was never cast in his plays. He would say things like, "Well, I would never tell someone not to go into drama but . . ." Even though I had done this feat of directing a three-act play as a senior in college, there was not much he said to me about the play except: "Nobody laughed during the death scene." That was the closest he ever came to complimenting me.

That year his wife started teaching Creative Drama and Children's Theater part-time. There were only a few of us in her class, but Jean McMillen was lively and supportive and fun. We did all kinds of creative exercises that expanded our imagination and how we saw the world. One of our assignments was to keep a journal and every day record something that related to each of the senses—seeing, hearing, smelling, tasting, and touching. We did brainstorming and improvisation. Although my competitive self sometimes got in the way, it nevertheless began to open my world into a broader sense of possibilities.

Jean had a good friend who taught Children's Theater at Northwestern University. I decided to apply to Northwestern for an MA in drama. Jean's letter of recommendation, together with my Cherub connection, got me in.

Acting Almost Does Me In; Directing Saves Me

Once again, I met my match when it came to the acting class. At Northwestern, graduate students had to get either a B or an A in every class or they would be kicked out of the graduate program. I got a C in acting, and clearly, I was in deep trouble. But there was a way out. If I got an A in another class I could stay. I took several classes that included writing and got A's in those classes.

I also took a directing class with some classmates who went into professional theater. One of them was Peter Strauss who became a very successful television actor in such miniseries as *Rich Man Poor Man*, *Masada*, *The Jericho Mile*, and *Soldier Blue*. We directed scenes in that class. If the class audience liked the scene, they applauded when it was finished, and if they didn't, they just sat there in a deep silence of disapproval. All of Peter's scenes were clapped for. Mine weren't.

I decided to go out on a limb for my next scene and do something very different that was either going to be a total failure or a success. I cast modern dancers and did a scene of a Greek chorus from one of the Greek plays. I had the dancers move around using modern dance movements and unusual vocal rhythms that I had learned in the Reader's Theater class as a Cherub. This included echoes and repetitions of one word or having half the chorus say one word and the rest make strange sounds. It was kinda "out there." The scene went up with the class watching. It finished. Silence.

And then a little more silence. Oh no! And then wild applause. A day later Peter came up to me to compliment me on that scene.

It must have made an impression on Peter because twenty-five years later when I asked if I could interview him for my book *The Collaborative Art of Filmmaking: From Script to Screen*, he agreed. We had a lovely lunch. He gave me a little kiss goodbye on the left cheek. How I remember that moment! When I had a follow-up question, he gave me his home phone number so I could call and we could talk after his children had gone to bed.

For our directing-class scenes, we cast actors from the acting class. Shelley Long (she later played Diane in *Cheers*) was one of them. I cast her in either two or three of the scenes I did that year. She was delightful. The guys could hardly concentrate on their own parts because she was so cute and perky. She knew how to handle them—and handle the part—and she was a good study and knew her lines and always did a good job.

In the fifteen years from 1965 to 1980, I directed about twenty-five different projects. Most of them were three-act plays, but some were Reader's Theater, and some of them were one-act plays. Many of them were directed at colleges where I taught, or at little theaters. Some were well known such as *The Diary of Anne Frank*, *You Can't Take It with You*, *The Fantasticks*, *The Visit*, and *The Madwoman of Chaillot*. I did Shakespeare's *Comedy of Errors* after *Star Wars* came out and set it in a galaxy far away. My servant twins were droids. We used music from *Star Wars*.

After graduate school and seminary, I was hired for $1,000 to direct *Fiddler on the Roof* for a summer production made up of high school and college students. If they paid $10 to be in the play I had to cast them. But there was plenty of room in the town of Anetevka for lots and lots of people. And everybody had at least one line.

Unpacking

Striving for a career in drama takes a whole lot of determination and gumption.

Everyone seems to think drama is about acting, and if you're not great at acting you need to give up and find a job where you can make a living. In spite of the conflict between my love for drama and the lack of skill in that area, love eventually won. I had two epiphany moments when I knew I had to remain in drama. I went to see the play *The Caucasian Chalk Circle* by Bertold Brecht at the Tyrone Guthrie Regional Theater in Minneapolis. The lead was played by Zoe Caldwell who was a stellar theater actress and was so brilliant that I decided I must remain part of that world. A few years later, while still trying to figure out how to do this, I went to see the play *Chorus Line* and once again decided somehow or another I would find a way to remain in drama. I just had to find my way, which I first did in seminary and then later in the film industry through script consulting.

Linda's Trivia

Favorite female character in a film: Carol from *As Good as It Gets*

Favorite male character in a film: Deputy Sam Gerarrd in *The Fugitive*

Chapter Five
Dr. Wayne Rood

It's not unusual for someone to have one great teacher in their life. A great teacher "gets" the student. They understand what is needed to bring out the good qualities in the student and give insights to the student that will guide them for the rest of their life. In a sense they create and build the person into who they become.

Dr. Wayne Rood was that person for me. He was my major professor at seminary—Pacific School of Religion (PSR). He was the head of the Religion and Arts Department, which included a section in religion and drama. I went to seminary because I wanted to explore the relationship of Drama and Religion and how Drama works with religious themes and images and communicates values. There were very few places in the world where I could study this subject. And there were very few schools with as much freedom as PSR.

I had no idea where this study would lead me, but I stepped out into this new world with faith and trust. This was one of the more difficult stages in my life because I had very little money. I lived on food stamps, a part time job at a church, and scholarships.

I intended to get a Certificate of Theological Studies which would take nine months, but I found seminary so exciting I stayed five years. I got a Master's degree and then a ThD—all because of Wayne. His classes were masterpieces. He got students emotionally involved. Sometimes we were brought to tears. Other times we were so frustrated as we tried to learn our new identity in terms of how we were defined as Christians and as artists.

He taught by exposing me to different ideas and by opening up opportunities for me, and I kept taking them. Sometimes it meant passing out tickets at a play or working the lights for a play or simply letting me know about plays I might want to go and see. He saw life much more broadly than my work at seminary and introduced me to theater and theater folk in the Bay Area.

In order to enter this program, each student had to be a practicing artist. They also had to take theology classes at the seminary and find the connection between religion and their art form. My focus was on drama with an emphasis on directing. Other students in the class included a sculptor who spent two years producing an astounding head of John the Baptist, complete with much research of his psychology and his purpose. Another student focused on the Passion Plays. Another focused on improvisational drama.

I was interested in theology and felt that underneath all great plays and movies was an idea that had the potential to inspire us, uplift us, and guide us. I wasn't interested in what is called religious drama, which are plays about religious people and saints, or the annual Christmas pageant. I was interested in secular drama that communicated good values without being

Pollyanna-ish or being so nice that there is no dimensionality.

Teaching Students Like Me

Students come in all varieties. I've read a bit about people like me and why we sometimes move against the stream and why teachers often don't know quite what to do with us. My way of thinking is called divergent thinking. Instead of looking for correct answers where convergent thinking has one right answer, divergent thinkers are interested in the infinite possibilities and creative answers where you are valued for thinking outside the box. There is a famous exercise in creativity where each student is asked to write down uses for a brick. Convergent thinking would lead most people to using a brick to build a house or a wall. Divergent thinkers might decide to put wheels on a brick and make it into a roller skate. If you're a brick layer you might use it to mount a diamond ring when you propose to the beautiful gal. Wayne understood that I needed the freedom to explore and do things differently.

He taught by letting me find my way and gently nudging me in one direction and then in another, perhaps suggesting a book to open my mind or encouraging me to try new ideas. This was true both in my developing theology and my developing creativity. Those of us in the arts confused the other teachers—and sometimes ourselves—but Wayne was not confused.

Wayne was not just interested in our projects. He believed strongly in the ethics behind our work and the discipline behind our creative process. He believed that the process was just as important as the result, and the process had to have integrity and had to care about all the people involved. When I was directing my dissertation project, which was a play, he would come to my rehearsals and wander back stage. I couldn't figure out what he was doing, but the prop master told me he was checking to make sure my cast and crew were happy working with me.

Developing Skills

I also went to seminary because I was trying to work on a number of skills I wanted to develop. I had already directed about fifteen plays, but I tended to be a dominating director. I told actors what to do and when they resisted me, I spoke louder. I decided that was not the best way to get the best out of people. So in seminary, I took classes in psychology and how to work with groups, and I began to soften. Of course, I was there also because I loved theology and wanted to learn more about how prayer helped us in our daily life, how to talk to people with different beliefs without proselytizing, and how to work *with* rather than *against* people. I wanted to lower my defenses. What I was looking for would not be found in most schools, but I found it in seminary.

The importance of what I learned became clear to me when the play I directed for my dissertation project, *The Visit* by Friedrich Dürrenmatt, had finished its nine-night run. I had a conversation with my technical director, Jack, who had seemed to be one of those egotistical theater people when he came on board with this production. I had been concerned because of his attitude, and I decided six weeks of rehearsal developing a good attitude with my cast had to be stronger than his ego. He thought he was the cat's meow and that he was going to show off his theater know-how. But as a result of the collaboration of my cast and their kindness, he started to mellow.

When the play was over, I called to thank him, and he said, "I have a question to ask you. I've been in a lot of theater, but I don't understand; why was this experience so different?"

I told him, "This was my doctoral dissertation project in the area of theater and theology, and the process was as important as the result."

He said, "I get it."

Jack also told me that he had fallen off the ladder while doing some of the tech work and had hurt himself badly enough that he was not able to go to work for a week. He mentioned that the leading actor had paid his rent for that month. I knew nothing about this going on behind the scenes, but I was so pleased. It showed me that the cast and crew really cared about each other. And it told me that what Wayne had set out to teach me had succeeded.

Right before I received my ThD, Wayne took me aside and gave me the best compliment I ever received: "I am really happy with who you have become. It was touch and go for a while, but you did it!" I had become a better person through this process, and I had developed values that would guide me for the rest of my life.

Unpacking

A good teacher might know how to teach but uses the same technique for everyone. This means it can be difficult to find your own path because you are constantly on a path that doesn't work for you. I have learned that a great teacher figures out how each student learns and what is needed to spark that person.

Once I had integrated what Wayne taught me, I could begin to design my own program and integrate required classes with projects and papers that reflected my interest. As I moved into script consulting, I could begin to collaborate with screenwriters who consulted with me. When I gave seminars, I learned how to nurture and motivate and inspire the students. I began to see my calling as nurturing creativity and spirituality. None of this would have happened without Wayne.

Linda's Trivia

Favorite play I directed: *The Visit* because I was finally able to help my actors find new layers of depth in their roles.

Part Two:
My Brilliant Career

Chapter Six
Starting My Life in the Film Biz

There are always events in life that are difficult. There are big struggles and the things that we have to do but wish we didn't. There are crises. Medical illnesses. Relationship breakups. Untimely deaths. People we have to put up with but wish we didn't. Sometimes life throws unexpected curve balls that hit us right in the gut.

I sometimes rank these events. What was really, really difficult? Which events went on and on and wore me down? Which events forced profanity and vulgarities out of my usually clean mouth? And which events were really hard but had a wonderful outcome?

Starting a business was one of the most difficult stages in my life. And yet, it was one of the best parts of my adult life, filled with good relationships, good creative energy from myself and clients, and opportunities to travel for seminars. I came in contact with very interesting clients—some of them famous and some of them average Joes.

The film business was challenging and demanded the patience of Job.

It Takes True Grit

When you grow up in a home that is filled with love and nurturing and positive energy, the film business can throw you for a loop. Of course it's difficult to get a job in any career. But getting into the film business, then staying in the film business, takes all the grit you've got. It's a business often driven by ego, power, and money. And yet some of the most talented and creative people can be found in this field and can make our career light up with joy.

When I entered the business in 1980, I had many strikes against me. I was mid-thirties, a female, and someone who had already had a career as a drama teacher. I could see that, in many cases, this was a business that wanted to nurture young men in their twenties.

The film business is practical. I discovered it didn't have a great deal of respect for people they considered over-educated. It was fine to have a BA degree, but anything above that was problematical. It implied your head was in the clouds, and you had studied things but not done things. I already had a BA, two MAs, and a ThD. That was not going to get me anywhere in the film business.

While applying for jobs and doing meet-and-greets in offices and at receptions, I tried to find jobs that would help me get by financially while trying to clear a path that would allow me to use my love of drama. Sometimes I typed and earned money for every word I typed. Sometimes I got jobs reading scripts for companies, but this was not a steady income and did not lead to any full-time work. At one point, I applied for a job selling pencils over the telephone, but the morning I was about to start work, I realized it was the last straw and was just one step above selling pencils on the street corner. I called the company and canceled my pencil-selling career.

I realized fairly quickly that my education was not going to pave the way for me to get a foot in the door. I sat down and figured out what the film business wanted that I had to offer. I took all my degrees off my resume except for my BA in English and I sold myself on my typing ability. I was really good. I typed seventy words a minute on a manual typewriter, and occasionally someone was gobsmacked by my ability.

Getting My Toe in the Door

I signed up for temp jobs, including signing up at the Personnel Department at Norman Lear's company. I received a call to come in for one day as a substitute to work for the director of development, Fern Field. After one day I was asked to come back for another day and another day and another day. I became the assistant to her assistant and typed and xeroxed. I ended up working as a temp for them from December 1980 until late Summer 1981.

This at least helped me get started, and I began to understand that a good way to get into this film business was to let all the ego go and enter the basement door. I tried to do well on everything I was asked to do. And I hoped that some opportunities and doors would open.

Finding a Role Model

Fern was an amazing role model for me. She was firm. Diplomatic. Got things done. Made things happen. Got down to brass tacks. In the most subtle way, she gave me opportunities to do things I would enjoy doing instead of only typing and xeroxing. When she produced the television movie *First Lady of the World* about Eleanor Roosevelt, she not only gave me the opportunity to read the script, which is something I loved doing, but one day she asked me to go to the library to find pictures of all the people mentioned in the script to help the casting director.

As a result of my research for Fern, word got around at the company that I was good at research, and other executives would sometimes ask if I could help them out. So I became kind of a floater and worked for other people as well.

When she produced the Emmy award-winning Afterschool Special called *The Wave*, she gave me the opportunity to be an extra pretending to be a high school student at an assembly.

When she produced the Afterschool Special *Don't Hit Me, Mom*, she asked me to bring various papers to the set. I began to notice that I was always dropping things off just before lunch and would be invited to stay for one of the very good catered meals. My meals at my apartment were cheap and minimal. The catered meals on the set were delicious and plentiful.

A Good Place to Work

Norman Lear's company was a very kind place to work. I was paid above minimum wage, which impressed me. Probably if a job had opened up, I would have moved into a full-time position since they promoted from within. Nothing was opening up, and I remained a temp day after day and month after month. But I had no benefits. At one point I became very ill and couldn't go to work for two days. One of the secretaries brought food for me, and another person had a brother who was an MD and brought him and bananas. When I returned to work, I had lost two days of wages. My budget was so carefully worked out that even losing some money put me in dire straits. I decided to write to the personnel department and explain the situation. I asked if there was a Compassion Clause in my contract that might give me two days of lost wages. They immediately wrote back and said they would pay me.

Fern's regular secretary, Susan, who I assisted, was one of the kindest and most generous and most-inclusive people I had ever met. Part of her job was to read scripts and let Fern know which ones were possibilities to produce. Susan didn't like to read scripts, and she and Fern worked it out that I would read them.

As an assistant, Susan had many unique jobs to do for Fern. One time she said to me, "Fern has this important person coming into town, and she wants to go to the play *The Little Foxes* with Elizabeth Taylor. But they're sold out. What should I do?"

I explained to Susan that a play is never totally sold out. There are always a few seats left, called "house seats" because they don't know if a really important person such as the President of the United States or the director of development of Normal Lear's company wants to see the play. These seats are usually around seventh-row center and some of the best seats in the house. I also explained to Susan that the trick to getting these seats was not to go through the box office but to the business office. Susan asked if I would take over, and I said, "Yes." Five minutes later I had two seats seventh-row center for her and her guest.

An Ending and a New Beginning

When the Writers' Strike hit that summer of 1981, there was no more work for me. Writers were not allowed to write, and there were no scripts to read and little administrative work to do. I got several other short-lived jobs reading scripts, but nothing was breaking through. I had gotten my toe in the door, but my foot was still stuck.

During this time, one of the writers who had been in discussion with Fern on his script, told me he knew his script had problems, but he didn't know what they were and didn't know how to solve them. Joe was at an impasse.

I suggested that I take my method of analyzing scripts that I had developed as part of my doctoral dissertation and apply it to his script to see if I could locate the problem. I read the script, analyzed the structure of the story, the story line, the characters, and the theme. I made notes and had a discussion with him, identifying the problem areas. He said to me, "I have struggled with this for five years and within one hour with you, I knew what to do."

Although the job ended with Fern in August 1981, I got a job reading scripts and writing reports at the Los Angeles Public Theater. That didn't last long either. The theater closed. I continued to do other piecemeal reading jobs. I then got a job at EMI films, reading twenty-five scripts a month for a thousand dollars. I could just make it, and that was fairly stable for a few months until EMI went under.

On September 17, 1981, as a last-ditch effort, I decided to place an ad in the Hollywood Reporter trade paper, wondering if other writers were in the same position as Joe had been. My ad read: "Having trouble selling a script? Stuck on a rewrite? Literary PhD can help."

I fibbed a bit which I generally don't do, but I knew a ThD in Religion in the Arts wouldn't give me any clients. This ad did.

I charged $35 a script and spent hours and hours analyzing the script on my own, and met with the writer for several hours, identifying the strengths and weaknesses and what do about them. And I began to get clients. One of the writers said, "There is no way I'm only going to pay you $35 for all of this work." He gave me $100 and it occurred to me that maybe I could raise my rates. I also did several scripts for well-known producers for free who then gave me an endorsement in exchange for my work. I managed to live on measly freelance wages because I moved into the back room of a friend's small bungalow in West LA and paid $200 a month for rent. I had my own room and kitchen privileges, and I also did some of the cleaning. I lived at Mary's house for about a year and a half until I met Peter, my future husband, and we moved in together.

Little by little, I got clients and squeaked by for about two years. Fern Field became one of my clients. She recounts why she came to me. "I was having trouble editing down the script, and I was feeling very stressed about it. I said to my husband Norman Brooks, 'If we sell this story, I want to hire Linda to help me with the editing.' And my husband, in his infinite wisdom, said, 'Wouldn't it be better to hire Linda now so we can make the sale?' And I was flabbergasted. 'Of course it would. Call Linda—Linda's a genius!' So, we did, and it was one of our most successful Afterschool Specials: *The Day My Kid Went Punk*. It sold almost immediately after our work with Linda and within a few weeks we were in production."

Over the years I had many fascinating clients like Fern. One of my clients was pardoned by Donald Trump for a campaign-finance crime he had committed. Part of his punishment included sleeping at the jail but being free during the day. We had to end our in-person meeting by 5 p.m. so he could report back to jail.

Another client had spent a year in a white-collar jail for trying to rob a bank. He told me that it was a bank on the second floor of a building, and he never made it back to the first floor before he was arrested.

One of my clients was an Academy-Award-winning actor. I never disclose client's names so I can't be more specific. Two other clients were Academy-Award-winning writers.

Clients came to me from all six continents and wrote in many different genres and styles. Some of the scripts were wonderful, and about one hundred were produced, including *The Never Ending Story 2*, *Universal Soldier*, *Luther*, and a number of films that won independent film awards.

From the beginning, I loved what I was doing but couldn't make a living at it without more clients. In 1983 I met Judith

Claire at a Women in Film function. Judith was a career consultant, and she was my miracle person who changed my career. Judith deserves her own chapter.

Unpacking

In retrospect, I've realized that this is a collaborative business. Nobody makes it alone. One never knows where the breaks will come from. In my business, sometimes they were a referral from well-known people in the business, but most of the time my breaks came from people not well known but generous and willing to share resources. They recommended me for script-consulting jobs. Sometimes they arranged seminars for me. They endorsed my work. They introduced me to people who were interested in hiring me or knew people who might hire me.

One of the most helpful people in my career was actor-director Tony Bill. He was known to be supportive of women in the industry. I consulted on his script for free, and he gave me an endorsement and allowed me to use his name when I wanted to meet people who I thought might be interested in my services. Tony seemed to know everybody in the business, and everybody liked him. If I wanted to meet the vice president of a studio, I would call Tony's office and ask the secretary if Tony was comfortable with me using his name and telling the executive that Tony suggested that I call. There was only one time when Tony asked me not to use his name. He was in a business relationship with someone and was in a critical negotiating stage. But all the other times he said, "Yes."

Another person, who was very helpful for me, was a woman from Women in Film in San Francisco—Karen Jacobs. Karen would not be considered successful in the usual ways. She wrote some screenplays, but most of them were not produced. She occasionally gave seminars in screenwriting, and sometimes she judged film festivals. But she was not a household name. Yet she was incredibly warm and friendly and generous. Wherever I went in the world, it seemed Karen knew somebody. This didn't always lead to jobs, but it led to social occasions that were high points of my travel. One woman she knew invited my husband and me to her home in Milan, Italy, when I was teaching there. Another took me on a lovely day trip in the countryside of Italy when I was visiting. Sometimes she recommended me for seminars or script-consulting jobs. She simply was all about generosity, and she taught me to value that trait and help other people's careers as she had supported mine. She also taught me that the breaks don't usually come from the big names. They come from the people like Karen, willing to share resources and appreciate good work and are kind and giving.

Linda's Trivia

Favorite traits found in my favorite people in the business: The ability to collaborate and support each other.

Chapter Seven
My Brilliant Career Consultant Judith Claire

Without Judith, I would not have had my career. I'm quite convinced about that.

At the beginning it seemed as if my business was starting to take off, but it really wasn't. I only had a few clients a month, which was not enough to sustain me. Originally, I started my business to make a name for myself. It occurred to me that if I became known for my abilities to analyze a script, studios and production companies might seek me out and offer me a job.

It didn't take long for me to realize that I was doing what I really wanted to do. I was a natural entrepreneur, although I didn't know it at the time. I was self-directed. I had no problem working hard. Once I committed to my freelance business, I turned my full attention to building my business and making consulting my career.

But what should I call myself? It was important that I had a title that would define me. My hairdresser asked me, "What will you be doing?"

I answered, "Consulting on scripts."

He said, "Then you're a script consultant."

That was easy.

Within months of starting my business I began to suspect that I was not going to be able to do this without some kind of a team around me. There were people in the business who had parents in the industry who got them jobs. There were people who knew powerful people. Not me. No connections at all. So, I struggled along for almost two years.

In those two years I started to create a team who could strengthen my weaknesses and help my business grow. I had very little money, but anything extra went back into the business. If I couldn't afford the $75 an hour to hire someone, I hired them for thirty minutes at $37.50. I took a class in time management. I worked with a marketing director to help me create a brochure and give me some marketing tips. I worked with another marketing person who helped me get my name out and who suggested I do some television interviews about my unique job. She sent me to a media consultant who taught me to be a good guest on television. I eventually ended up with an appearance on CNN, Good Morning New York, National Public Radio, and Good Morning L.A. All of this was done on a shoestring budget by turning over every nickel and eating cheaply.

Around this time, I went to an evening workshop led by the President of the Los Angeles Chapter of the National Organization of Women Business Owners (NOWBO). The woman who led it, Marsha (not her real name), told us to practice saying what we do in our jobs in one sentence. The sentence had to fulfill a need, and it had to be clear enough that if people had that need, I would be the obvious person to hire. I understood the importance of this because I occasionally met people who were so vague about their work, I had no idea what they did. I knew a woman for years who said, "I'm in media," and I never figured out her job, so of course I could never hire her. There were other people who were too broad in their descriptions that they would tell me, "I write and direct and produce," but I had no idea what they had done and what experience they had and what they were selling.

After playing around with this, my sentence became: "I'm a script consultant, and my job is to identify, analyze, and help solve elusive script problems." By that time, I knew that one of the problems writers have is the inability to identify what are the problems in their script.

What Did Judith Teach Me?

When I started working with Judith, she suggested I do a survey of writers and ask them what problems they encounter when they get stuck. She asked, "What language do they use to describe the difficulties they have?" The idea was to find the word that described the problem and use that word in my advertising. The word that kept coming up was "objective." Writers said there is a time that they get too close to their material and they can't see it clearly anymore. They are not objective about it, yet it's their darling baby. Judith then told me to identify myself as an "objective" professional in my advertising. That is clearly what they needed.

Judith added another layer to this understanding. She said, "Do another survey and find out where people go when they're stuck on a script. Who do they go now for feedback?"

The answer from most was friends, sometimes a writer's workshop, sometimes their favorite aunt or uncle, somebody they met at a party, or perhaps they know somebody in the business who might know somebody who knows somebody. Maybe they have a cousin who works props and thinks their script is marvelous, or they met somebody who is breaking into acting and somehow believe they must know about scripts and can help them solve the script problems and sell their script. They might even put in a good word to some other actor who might know somebody who knows somebody.

What was missing was a professional that was accessible to any writer who wanted help on their script. If a script has sold, the writer works with the development executive at a studio or a production company. If the executive is good at their job, the problem gets solved but some executives may be focused on casting or the budget or story or character but may not know how to solve the problems. If the script has not sold, the writer often has no professional who can help them make it better.

Judith suggested I ask another question in my survey: "What kind of feedback do you get from people who read your script?" Usually it was something like, "Love it, but it seemed to drag in the middle." Or, "I just couldn't get into it, but I guess I don't like comedies." Or, "It's really great. It should make a whole lot of money." But that wasn't helping them solve the multiple problems a script can have.

Do I Have the Skills?

Judith then asked me many questions about what I was bringing to my new business. First, she wanted to know what my skill level was. I talked about all the drama classes I had taken and the work I had done as a reader of scripts and plays I had directed. I had a BA in English and an MA in drama and an MA in religion and the arts and a ThD in drama and theology. I had studied this subject for years. I discussed the clients I already had and the method I developed for my doctoral dissertation to help me analyze a script.

She prodded me to make a long list in our meeting. Every time I ran out of ideas, she would encourage me to come up with other skills I had. I included the school play my junior and senior years in high school, and my time as a Cherub at Northwestern University. I discussed specific work I had done with teachers in college and graduate school, as well as conferences I'd attended in drama. She helped me understand that I had skills for this business. I had something to contribute that was new and innovative that might help writers solve writer's problems.

Then she asked me a very unexpected question: "If there was another person who was exactly as skilled as you are, what kind of qualities as a human being do you bring that would encourage a screenwriter, a producer, or director to come to you and not go to the other person who is equally qualified?"

That was a toughie at first since it meant that I had to think of really good things about me, but I began my list: "I'm nurturing. I learned that from my mother. She encouraged others, and I have learned to do that as well."

She pushed me to come up with other qualities. "I'm diplomatic. I took classes in college and graduate school in psychology, interpersonal relationships, and group process. During my time in seminary, I worked with my major professor, Dr. Wayne Rood, on ways to work with actors so I was able to pull good things out of them without being controlling or manipulative. I do the same with my clients."

Every time I stopped, Judith would say, "Tell me more." I talked about qualities such as generosity, being a nice Midwesterner, being a spiritual person who tried to respect others, and having an ability to be very focused on my work. All of these things got added to this long list.

Judith then said, "This is worth something." She helped me get over my belief that I was not up to the job or could only charge a small amount of money. She helped me understand that all the preparation I had done to develop this skill, together with my natural qualities, was a very good thing and I truly had something to sell.

She also helped me understand I had to price myself for the market as opposed to what the service was worth. My work might have been worth $1500, but writers might only be willing to pay $50 or $100. I had to be affordable. Eventually I had a number of services so the writer would pay more if they wanted more detail or if they wanted a longer meeting.

I continued to see my friend Marsha during this time, and her advice reinforced what Judith was telling me. Marsha explained to me, "If you aren't losing 10 percent of your business because you're too expensive, you are probably priced too cheaply. You aren't supposed to be able to sell to everyone, but you should be able to sell to most of the people who contact you."

I became smart about money and began to price various services depending on how much detailing the client wanted or could afford. I wanted a service to fit whatever pricing the clients had in their heads. If they could only afford $50, I still wanted to be able to give them something. If they could afford $5,000, they would get an extremely detailed analysis that included line-by-line as well as overall analysis of the story and the character and the theme and the images. Even at the end of my career, after almost forty years, I had one service that was only $50 and included looking at a paragraph that explained the story line. One client couldn't believe that I would charge $50 for a paragraph about their story, and I said, "You could have your aunt read it and tell you it's wonderful, but if I read it, you're going to get lots of information about that idea." He did hire me and said that he definitely got a lot of good information that made it possible for him to continue developing his story.

Judith and My Attitude Adjustment

Judith helped change my attitudes. I noticed as I became successful, a number of people wanted to go into business with me. I learned this is not an uncommon thing. Some people wanted to write treatments of the writer's scripts, and they wanted me to partner with them and add them as a component of my business. Others wanted to help me market the script. I would call Judith for her advice, and she would say, "They don't have anything to offer your business. You're focused on the art and craft of the script. Keep your focus."

Judith helped me keep my head on straight and not be silly about things such as money.

I once told Judith that I did not expect to ever earn more than $36,000 a year. Judith responded appropriately—she laughed. She said, "You're going to do far better than that, so you may as well start getting used to it." And I did learn to deal with money and to be smart and not stupid.

Dealing with Competition

I felt very competitive and very threatened as other people started to consult on scripts. My success had motivated them. But I didn't want competition. Judith explained to me that competition was a good thing. She said it normalizes going to a script consultant because there are a number of them out there. I began to welcome competition and to understand that other script consultants often focused on other areas of the script. We were really not doing the exact same thing. Several of us began to recommend others for jobs and even had a breakfast group where we would welcome new consultants who came on the scene. Some focused on marketing, some on the psychology of character, and some focused on other genres such as science fiction and detective shows. It took me years to overcome my competitive attitude, but with Judith's help, I did.

Ethical Adjustments

I learned the downside of being in business. There were clients who tried to cheat me in one way or another. At the beginning of my business, the client would give me the script, and I would write the report and prepare for our one-on-one meeting. We would meet. The client was to pay me when we finished the meeting. Sometimes clients would forget their checkbooks. Sometimes they said they would mail me a check in a few days. Sometimes they would tell me I would get paid when they got paid, which might have been never.

Judith explained that it is very easy for us to become victims of people's unethical standards. A business transaction is an exchange of value for services rendered. I do the report and someone gives me money. They might also give me something else of value—early in my career I did trades which included a handmade quilt and a marble-topped table. The value has to be relatively equal and agreed upon by both people. This is called an exchange, and it needs to be ethical. Unethical behavior can lead to suffering from other people's bad business practices and to the stress that comes when people tell you the check is in the mail, but it isn't. I learned that being a victim meant spending an inordinate amount of time being a bill collector and a judge of character when those were not a part of my qualifications. Being a victim led to roiled up stomachs and sometimes anger and defensiveness. Judith taught me that I could have a business and feel really good most of the time. She taught me that I didn't have to put up with this and taught me how to handle victimizing circumstances.

Sometimes writers got defensive. Even though I was known for my ability at diplomacy, they weren't ready to hear any critique. As a result, out of the 2,500 projects I worked on in my career, eight people asked for their money back. They hired me to critique the script but didn't like being critiqued. At first, I just automatically refunded their money until I realized they were not responding to my integrity with their integrity. They had seen a critical remark and immediately got defensive. I began to tell these few clients that they needed to read the report at least three times over several days and apply some of the advice I had given them. If my suggestions didn't help the script, then I would refund their money. Each time this happened and the client went back to re-read the report, they apologized profusely. They needed to take the report seriously in the same way I had taken their script seriously.

Judith also helped me analyze personalities of my clients. Some were takers and not givers. Some were scoundrels. Some people were toxic, and I needed to do the work and then disengage. When I ran into problem areas, Judith was only a phone call away. I continued to meet with her periodically to handle problems as they came up.

The Spurts and Growth of a Business

Judith also taught me to analyze what was happening in my business. Was it growing? She taught me that the goal was affluence and abundance—for the business to be doing well and having enough money to live a good life and to also be able to reinvest in the business. She helped me understand the source of my success. Once she asked me that question, and I said I didn't know. She told me to look at my list of my clients from the last two months and I saw that 85 percent of them were recommended from somebody in the Women and Film organization. Judith told me to go to every Women in Film meeting and have my business cards with me. Judith explained that once you know the source of your success, continue to do the same actions that are making you successful. She said, "Don't live on hope and guesswork; look at the data." She also taught me not to be a taker and not to just look at others in terms of what they can give me but to be a giver with them as well.

She helped me analyze when my business was in trouble and what to do about it. There were two danger signs. Of course, I was in danger when I would go weeks without a client. At those times it was important to keep doing what had made me successful in other months. The other danger point was a sudden spurt of growth in my business. The temptation was to believe this would continue when it might not. There is a temptation to go and spend money on those things you have been wanting such as the new stereo set or the new dress. But then the next month might not go as well.

The goal was to normalize affluence, so the spurt in the business stabilizes. As my business grew—even though it was a freelance business—eventually my income stayed about the same month after month and year after year. I was living in affluence. Judith also taught me when there was a spurt in the business, to reinvest in the business so that it keeps growing.

She pointed out that the people who were there for me at the beginning of my career and believed in me enough to come for help, should always have some access to me. Others suggested to me that I have one pricing system for studios and production companies and another pricing system for writers who usually didn't have as much money. I rejected that idea because I believed that the client was paying for the work, and I wasn't going to charge some clients one amount and other clients a different amount. I also learned there are poor producers and wealthy screen writers. My job was not to assess how wealthy they were, but to do the work and charge the same amount to everyone. She taught me to respect all my clients whether they were famous, unknown, rich, or poor.

Judith and I have remained friends since 1983. She is humble enough to always be surprised when I tell her how influential she has been. And she is dear enough and generous enough to tell me, "You did it!"

Unpacking

A business doesn't just happen. It needs to be nurtured like a child and goes through different stages. It was easy to believe my business was just happening rather than that I had some control over its direction. It's easy to sit back and let things unfold, hoping all will go well. I discovered that most of us who start a business don't know what we're doing. Most of the time, we weren't business majors in college. We didn't grow up in our parent's business and take it over and inherit it. Many times we believe there is a conflict between doing well and doing good. Judith encouraged my ethical principles, and I discovered that being fair and honest actually prospered my business.

I gave birth to this new business which did not exist before. Since I was a pioneer in this field, it meant there were many situations where I could not look to others to help me. I learned to be open to advice and suggestions and began to see myself as an entrepreneur.

One of the keys to my success was creating a team to help me at each step of the way. Judith and Marsha were a part of that team and so were other teachers and consultants.

Before I began my business, there were screenwriters' workshops and classes and screenwriting groups. These didn't tend to be one-on-one, but occasionally a teacher would meet individually with students like I did—most of the work was focused on classes and advice between teacher and student.

In the films of the 1930s and 1940s there is occasionally a script consultant or script editor credit. In contemporary television series there is usually a script editor credit. These people are doing something similar to the job I created, but they are working for the company as opposed to an entrepreneur who is hired by the individual writer, producer, or director. Usually, these script editors are also writers. I was a script consultant who deliberately wasn't a screenwriter because I felt the skills were different, and I had an advantage of not having any investment in that script as a writer. I was never trying to rewrite but was there to help solve script problems. If there was a myriad of problems, I wanted to make sure to catch them all.

There are now hundreds of independent script consultants throughout the world. I deliberately trained competition for myself—teaching my method to seventy-five different people from seven different countries, which included Germany, Austria, Italy, Denmark, Sweden, Norway, and New Zealand. There are more than one hundred script consultants in Germany, and they occasionally even have a script-consultant convention. The job has now been normalized and stabilized, and a number of people are making money at this job. Judith was the master that helped me create and define this new business.

Linda's Trivia

The key to my success: Teamwork and the ability to find good people to help me and to somehow or another find the money to pay them.

Chapter Eight
The Perks of Teaching Seminars

The 1980s was a time of growing my script-consulting business and beginning to do seminars. The seminar industry was starting to be a big thing. It wasn't just all the relational seminars like EST and Loving Relationship Training. It was also seminars in specific areas of expertise. Historically, screenwriters had an attitude there was nothing to learn; you just had to be creative and write the script. But that attitude began to change in the early 1980s. Even those who thought they had nothing to learn about screenwriting began to feel that a seminar might do them some good. Syd Field was already doing screenwriting workshops. Robert McKee had just begun to teach, and hundreds came to his classes. Other teachers began to focus seminars on marketing the script, deal making, and low-budget film making.

Breaking into the Seminar Business

I was not new to teaching. I had already taught for two years at Grand Canyon College in Phoenix, one year at McPherson College in Kansas, and two years at the University of Laverne, Laverne, CA. I also taught in the prison system in southern California. The University of Laverne had the contract to supply teachers to the prisons. I taught humanities at the women's prison, at a medium security prison where prisoners had been at maximum security prisons in places like San Quentin, and I taught prisoners who had committed nonviolent crimes, mainly drug crimes where prisoners were there for one to two years.

I was already an experienced teacher and presumably a good one since I missed being Teacher of the Year by one vote at McPherson College. Nevertheless, I thought I was finished with teaching. But writers I met kept asking when I was going to teach my method that seemed to be so helpful to script-consulting clients.

I resisted seminars until the mid-1980s. I wanted to be a script consultant who occasionally did seminars rather than a seminar leader who occasionally did script consulting. I didn't want to produce my own seminars which some of my colleagues were doing. They had to market their seminars, find a venue, and arrange for support staff. Instead, I wanted organizations to produce my seminars, which as it turned out, they did. I sometimes pitched seminar ideas to organizations, and sometimes organizations sought me out. I gave seminars for Women in Film, The Directors Guild of America, Writers Guilds in the United States and in Europe and Australia, the American Film Institute, and the University of Wisconsin in Milwaukee and Madison, Wisconsin. I did seminars for executives at ABC, CBS, NBC, Tandem/TAT (Norman Lear's Company), the Walt Disney Company, as well as Turner Network Television. Some of these were one evening or one hour talks and some were several days.

As a college teacher, I usually taught on the semester system, but these short-term seminars were different. They were marathons. Typically, seminars were one-to-three days long, starting around 9:30 a.m. and finishing around 5 or 6:00 p.m. They were exhausting, but the saving grace in doing a seminar on film was showing film clips, which not only gave a break for the teacher but were a joy to watch over and over again as I explained the important concepts to learn from these great films.

I learned a valuable lesson at Turner Network which was based in Atlanta. I arrived and went to the Omni Hotel where I was staying and where the class was to be held. I did my one-day seminar, ate all of my meals at the hotel, and then flew back after the seminar was over. I returned home and realized the only thing I had seen in all of Atlanta was the Omni Hotel. I told myself how stupid that was to be starting a career and working in interesting places and not enjoying them. I decided that from then on, I would stay at least an extra day or two and sometimes longer to enjoy the sights.

Other Seminars

One of my early seminars was for UCLA. It was a good starting point, and UCLA and the Writers Guild decided to co-produce my seminar. Eight hundred people signed up. We needed to divide the seminar into two different weekends with about 400 people in each class because the room wasn't big enough for 800. It wasn't lost on me that the $10 fee for the seminar might have been responsible for the large numbers. All the poor writers could come as well as those who could afford the higher-priced seminars.

Various writers and colleagues started recommending me to film festivals and universities. I received a call from the Attorney General of California asking me to give a seminar for the media department of law enforcement. How could they make their small documentaries more interesting? For that seminar, I was recommended by my colleague Robert McKee who had turned down that assignment. The American Film Institute started hiring me to do seminars and sent me to a number of cities, including New York and Washington, DC. The University of Wisconsin at Milwaukee found out about me and started sending me to cities such as New York, Chicago, Washington, DC, Milwaukee, and Orlando. Other invitations came from Dallas, Austin, Tucson, and Hawaii, among others. In Madison, Wisconsin, the local PBS channel decided to make a little seven-minute TV movie of me—the girl from Peshtigo, Wisconsin, who made good. They followed me around for two days as if I were a movie star. I thought it was great fun.

The seminars were similar in most cases although sometimes I finessed them for the particular group. I usually dealt with how to tell a story, how to structure the story, how to create dimensional characters, how to develop a theme and ideas, and how to visualize the storyline through images. I talked about conflict and twists and turns and creating that big finish.

I also did a seminar for a short-lived sitcom with Mary Tyler Moore called *The Mary Show* and a seminar for the *MacGyver* series.

Working on *MacGyver*

MacGyver was one of my favorite seminars. They had an unusual problem; they were between their fourth and fifth season, and they were highly successful. But they were running out of ideas on how to keep the show going. In preparation for the seminar, I emailed the writers and asked them what they considered the major problems. I also asked them to send me a DVD of what they considered their best episode and what they considered their worst episode and what the network considered their best. I also asked them to send me the bible of the entire series so I knew all of the storylines that had been done. Our seminar was held in Palm Springs, and I was told I would have been flown first class if the plane had first class, but it was a small plane. I was given the name of my hotel and told that someone would pick me up at the airport.

When I got off the plane, I didn't see anybody who looked like they were looking for me, so I started walking toward a taxi cab. A young woman stopped me and introduced herself as one of my hosts. I turned around and right behind her was a limousine. I took one last look at the taxi and followed her prompting. The limousine would do just fine.

The group expected me to help them come up with a few ideas for more storylines, but instead, I wanted to give them concepts where each concept would lead to a number of new ideas. I read the bible for their whole series and analyzed how MacGyver entered the story in all their episodes. He was a tricky character because he wasn't a detective who was assigned to a case, nor a lawyer or anyone else who was assigned a case to solve. He had to keep falling into different types of cases. And just how often can someone stumble on a case?

I discovered they were using the same devices over and over again to connect him with various kinds of peril. I suggested that we find overall concepts where there could be many possible episodes out of one concept. I mentioned that in the series *Murder She Wrote*, Jessica entered the story through her acquaintances and relatives. We brainstormed different ways of entering the story—perhaps through a vacation or through a skill MacGyver had or a hobby. We began writing these concepts on newsprint and pasting the newsprint all over the walls. We then started brainstorming some individual episodes that could come from each concept.

Several writers told me they wanted their female characters to be more dimensional. I discussed several different techniques, and one of the producers objected. He thought the female characters were just fine. I mentioned that several writers had confidentially asked me to address this. Would he like me to share my ideas? Of course he said *yes*. I discussed several different techniques such as giving the female a skill to solve a particular part of the problem. It would be a skill MacGyver didn't have but needed. I suggested bringing in female characters of different ages to dimensionalize the series because characters of different ages have different ideas.

Teaching Abroad

During this time, my seminars were growing, and other colleagues also began teaching. Some of them were teaching abroad, so I tried to figure out how to make that happen for me. My husband and I were going to New Zealand for vacation in 1987, and it was just a hop, skip, and a jump to go to Australia and do a seminar and break into the international field. I hired somebody to figure out who would want me for a seminar in Australia if I more or less landed on their doorstep. The plan worked. I taught for the Australian Film and Television School and went to Sydney and Melbourne. I was then invited to New Zealand the following spring.

Somehow a producer in Rome, who started producing seminars, got wind that there was another seminar leader out there, and he invited me to Rome and London that same year. While in London, my host introduced me to an agent who was starting to produce seminars in Europe. He got me a job at the Pilots Writers Conference in Sitges, Spain, where I spoke a number of times over the next few years. Within this seminar were teams from all over Europe—Germany, Iceland, Scandinavia, France, Poland, Austria, Belgium, Switzerland, and Italy. My job was to do a three-hour talk and to meet for twenty minutes with ten teams that included the writer, the producer, and sometimes the director. I was to have read their scripts or treatments and give notes. After the first year they invited me back and asked me to do thirty minutes with each group with a director as well.

The conference was held at a hotel on the Mediterranean, and we held our group meetings and classes in rooms that contained replicas of some of the greatest sculptures and paintings in the world. An intricately carved fireplace was behind me, and my lecture podium faced the Mediterranean Sea.

These teams would then go back to their countries and mention they had enjoyed my seminar, so I began being invited to many different places, first in Europe and eventually in Africa, South America, the Middle East, and the Far East.

In 1987, my first book *Making a Good Script Great* was published. The book opened up the world to me. I gave the book as a gift when we were in southern New Zealand on vacation, staying on a sheep farm. The sheep farmers sent the book to somebody they knew who worked in television in Wellington. The writers there passed the book around and then sent the book to writers in Auckland. The New Zealand Film Commission invited me to come to do a three-week seminar one year after I had given away that book.

Somehow or other, that book got passed around in many places around the world. Some writers bought it when they came to the United States and shared it. Soon publishers from other countries contacted me and wanted to translate the book. The book continued to lay the foundations for seminars all over the world.

Eventually I did seminars and worked in more than thirty countries on six continents. Here is the alphabetical list: Argentina, Austria, Australia, Belgum, Brazil, Bulgaria, Canada (Alberta, British Columbia, Nova Scotia, Ontario, Saskatchewan), Colombia, Denmark, Dubai, Egypt, England, Finland, France, Germany (East Germany & West Germany), Indonesia, Ireland, Italy, Japan, Latvia, Mexico, New Zealand, Norway, Poland, Portugal, The Philippines, Russia, Singapore, South Africa, Spain, Switzerland, and Ukraine. Besides this list of seminars, I did some related work in China, Thailand, and Greece, as well as a Zoom seminar with Ecuador.

I gave the first professional screenwriting seminar in the former Soviet Union in 1991, shortly after the fall of the Berlin Wall. I was told there was no KGB in my class which was presumably great progress and delighted the writers. I wasn't sure whether to believe them, but it didn't matter. I didn't say anything controversial, and I didn't make any false moves.

Most of the time when I visited countries, I went early to get over jet lag and stayed an extra few days since it was such a privilege to have this opportunity to visit so many places. I experienced the culture and the people and saw the city through the eyes of insiders who lived there.

I had much to learn about different cultures and what was appropriate and what was not. I learned to email my host and ask the important question, "What am I going to do that I shouldn't do, so you can warn me ahead of time, and I'll make sure not to do it?" In Egypt it was recommended that I didn't drink alcohol because I was working for a Christian organization in a Muslim society. Then my host added, "But you can have a glass of wine at the hotel," which I did. And another student usually joined me.

In South Africa, where I team-taught with Carolyn Miller, we were told that it was dangerous to walk across the street from our five-star hotel. The zoo was just across the street, but we would need to have a car drive us if we wanted to go to the zoo.

In Cape Town we were told we could walk to a restaurant two blocks away on the main road, but we should not take the parallel road. We did a tour of Soweto which included Nelson Mandela's home, and we were told we would be safe if we had a Black guide and a Black driver.

In Berlin, several times I was at a train station with one bare lightbulb lighting the platform, and I asked my host if we were safe. She said, "Yes." We would walk down dark streets in Berlin, and she kept reassuring me we were fine. I learned to depend on the advice from my host, and I followed it to the letter.

The Russian Adventure

I might have learned some of the best lessons from my trip to Russia. The Berlin Wall had fallen just two years before in 1989, and Russia was feeling a rush of freedom and excitement interacting with other cultures. A group called the US Soviet Film Initiative in Los Angeles began bringing Russians in the film industry over to the United States and then sending at least one delegation during that time to Russia. That one delegation included several Academy-Award-winning writers such as Paul Schrader, writer of *Taxi Driver*, and Frank Pierson, writer of *Dog Day Afternoon*.

When the Russian Delegation came to the US, Peter and I were among the small group of people who hosted them. We visited Universal Studios with the Soviets and other US delegates, such as Dennis Weaver from *Gunsmoke* (who got us much attention wherever we went) and Michael Farrell from *MASH*. Each time the Russians came—which was approximately three times—someone in the Russian delegation would say to me, "It would be great if you could come and do a seminar in Russia." I thought it would be great also, but no one from the US was inviting me.

I had a friend working in the office of the American side of this film initiative, and she told me, "Linda, you're not famous enough for the US side to invite you. I suggest you get the Russians to invite you directly, and bypass the US side of this film initiative. When all the details are in place, then let the

US side know you are going, and let them be a little shocked."

The plans began. Using the contacts I had made when the Russians came to the US, I began faxing them about a possible seminar. Soon there were faxes back and forth, and I began to suspect that there was just one fax machine in Russia because the only time I could to get a fax through was two in the morning their time which was 2 p.m. our time. The plan began to take shape. But there was a hitch—I had to pay my way to Russia, but they would give me some rubles when I arrived and host me. I was going to be in London to do a seminar. We decided I would pay for my plane ticket from London to Moscow and do the two seminars side by side.

In retrospect it's hard to believe how lucky I was to do this trip. I had very little information. Someone was going to pick me up at the Moscow airport, but I didn't know who. That person would take me to the place I was staying, but I didn't know where that place was. There would be writers from around the former Soviet

Union at the seminar—including writers from such faraway places as Uzbekistan and the country of Georgia, as well as from Moscow. The seminar would be held every day from 9 a.m. until 1 p.m. I didn't know if there would be plans for the afternoon.

I still can't believe I said *yes* to all of this vagueness. But I did say *yes* because that was my natural inclination, and I wanted to open up the world to me. After all, I was still a Midwesterner looking for adventure.

Before I left for Moscow, I was told to bring several cartons of Marlboros in my suitcase because this is how taxi cabs were negotiated. If you held up a packet of Marlboros, a taxi would stop. For the first time in my life, I bought three cartons of Marlboros and carefully put them in my suitcase.

I was very nervous that morning in London because I had no idea what I was getting into. For a moment I thought of canceling everything, but that was not my nature. I flew to Moscow, got to the airport, and was picking up my bags but still had no idea how I would find this person I was supposed to meet. My seat partner was standing next to me in the luggage area and said, "I think that woman over there is looking for you." She was holding up a sign with one hand that had my name on it and was carrying flowers with the other hand. Her name was Olga, and she was my translator, my minder, my protector, and my constant companion. I immediately let Olga know I had Marlboros to be used as needed.

I saw the first set of negotiations which involved who was going to drive us out of the airport and how many packets of Marlboros it would take. One of my hosts was in charge of the negotiations. There was the walking away and walking back in careful thought and much eyeing of the Marlboros. The stakes were high. Within a few days, I figured out my host would try to give out the least number of Marlboros to get a ride because he figured that at the end of my time, he'd get whatever Marlboros were left. So negotiations were lengthy with a certain amount of fervor and passion.

Somewhere after the taxi ride from the airport, we got into another car driven by a screenwriter. As we were driving to the retreat center, police stopped our car and the driver quickly said to me, "Don't say a word." Supposedly the driver had gone through a stop sign. Where we were going was near an armament factory, and Americans were not allowed in that area. Naturally I stayed very mum. I figured out that it was best not to go anyplace by myself and to always depend on my Russian hosts. After the second day, I had a driver who would take Olga and me on excursions in the afternoon.

I was given the best room at the retreat center, which meant I had beautiful views of the birch trees, and I had a toilet and a sink as part of my room. Olga informed me that the shower inside the retreat center was not good enough for me, so every day we went to the spa where tea in a beautiful Russian samovar was put out for us, plus towels, and the shower even had hot water.

When I was not teaching, Olga and my driver would take me on adventures. I was given a tour of Moscow, as well as the outlying towns and cultural activities. I was dropped off by Olga and my driver to see the Bolshoi ballet, which was actually a variety show that night. They told me they would pick me up after the show. They also said someone from their group would come and sit next to me. That person was a "no show." I hoped someone would find me and pick me up. I was being sustained by faith and trust and hoped I was not being foolhardy.

I had learned enough Russian to order champagne, ask where my seat was, and check my coat. When the performance was over, it occurred to me I had seen hundreds of cars outside and thousands of people inside and wondered what I would do if I couldn't find Olga and my driver. No worries. Olga found me.

Conditions in Russia

Food was not scarce but variety was. Olga explained that the problem was the supply chain. She said there was plenty of food but that they often couldn't get supplies through. So, if the kitchen got a load of carrots, we would eat carrots until another vegetable came along. One morning there was no coffee. Sometimes we had baked apples for several nights in a row. I realized in retrospect there was so much heart from everyone, including the kitchen staff, who were clearly honored to have an American as a guest. They wanted so much to please me. A number of times the cook would ask if I was happy with the food. I later learned that I could have asked for specific types of eggs, and they would have made them for breakfast.

I was gracious, but I felt their hearts were bigger than mine. I was thankful, but I felt I should have been overcome with gratitude because I realized I was the first American most of them had ever met. I had learned enough Russian to greet everyone I saw in their own language, including staff and participants, and that helped with our connection.

Since I was the guest, I was an insider. That meant that I was invited to the head writer's room each evening with other top writers. Suddenly there was food including salami, cheese, bread, and vodka. Supposedly this was all black-market food and was more than we had at other meals. Most of the people in this invitation-only room had a good working knowledge of English.

I was expected to sit at the head table for meals. I consulted on several of their treatments which had been translated for me. I was given a gift of an original painting and was told to tuck it in the bottom of my suitcase and not declare it. The painting had been done by a prisoner in Siberia whose hands were crippled except when he painted. I was told it was quite valuable. It has hung in our dining room for more than thirty years.

Communication was difficult because there seemed to be only one phone in the building. Unexpectedly it turned out a friend of mine—Lindsay Smith who wrote the foreword to these memoirs—was also in Moscow at the same time shooting her film. Lindsay informed me that someone else we knew was in Moscow and throwing a party. Susie had not been able to reach me to invite me, but Lindsay assured me I was invited.

I just had to find a way to get there, and my driver was happy to drive me. Lindsay explained to me that somehow, in spite of poor communication systems, everything seemed to work out well. Everyone got to where they were supposed to be.

I also spoke at a university screenwriting class. The teacher had deliberately chosen a smaller classroom in case fewer people showed up, so I would not be embarrassed. So many showed up they were sitting on the radiators, the floors, and sharing desks. They gave me a beautiful headscarf as a gift.

One of the highlights was staying a night at Olga's parents' apartment in Moscow, a weekend when they were gone. It was Stalin grey, and it might have been considered one of the better apartments in Moscow. Olga slept on the sofa, and I got her parents' bed for the night.

This was the beginning of my overseas adventures, which were to continue for more than thirty years.

My Gracious Hosts

It wasn't until I had ventured on more trips that I became aware of this heart connection that happened almost every time. I brought gifts along for my host on all my trips, and I sometimes thought about how I could be as gracious to the people I met as they were to me. I sometimes thought about what I might have done differently. I might have gone out of my way to thank the staff and shake their hands. In some situations, I might have asked for a tour of the kitchen and to meet the staff who cooked for me. I might have offered to take my host out to dinner. I was kind and nice, but in retrospect, I don't feel I was gracious enough to really receive fully their hearts and give my heart back. I don't think anyone saw me as a failure at graciousness, but I feel I could have done more.

With all the traveling, I found most of my hosts to be wonderful people. They typically planned cultural activities for me. I saw the Lipizzaner horses perform in Austria. The Vienna Boys Choir also sang at that same performance.

In Australia I was taken to the seaside. I had to be there by 8 p.m. We sat down on bleachers and stared at the water. I had no idea what I was looking for. At exactly 8 p.m. 800 knee-high penguins marched out of the water to find resting places on the land at night. I was delighted.

I saw folk dancing in Ukraine, a tango performance in Argentina, where the lead dancer danced a little tango with me. I visited the Swarovski Crystal exhibition hall. They had life-size horses that were made of crystals. There were also waterfalls and Elvis exhibits, all made from crystals.

In Spain, my host asked if I would like to see a Spanish tuna. I thought it was a strange request but since I like to say *yes* to most things I said, "Yes." I expected to see some kind of strange fish. But a Spanish tuna is a group of men from the various colleges who sing. They sing for people's retirements, birthdays, and other occasions. In this case, they were singing for someone's retirement in the courtyard. My host invited them to sing at our dinner that night. I was traveling with a colleague, Carolyn Miller, who was working on a Spanish script, and told her about the treat we were going to have that evening. After dinner in the private dining room, they sang love songs and asked us to dance. Carolyn was somewhat embarrassed, but I reminded her that this is not something that usually happens to women our age—we were in our fifties, and we should glory in it.

I saw art museums and historical museums and drove in the countryside and wandered through Old Towns. In South Africa, I enjoyed a horseback ride by the ocean on a thoroughbred horse who was awfully fast and rather scary. In Thailand I rode an elephant. In Egypt I rode a camel. The person leading the camel asked if I wanted to gallop in the Sahara. At first, I thought it might be fun, but then I realized the plan would be for him to sit behind me on the camel. I quickly realized where his hands might go—and decided I did not need to gallop in the Sahara on a camel.

I turned my sights to the Arabian horses and told my host, "Tell the horse guide I don't want to just walk my horse. Tell him

I'm a pretty good rider and would like to gallop."

The guide agreed. I started to trot, and he whispered to me, "Wait until we're on the other side of the dunes."

I understood he didn't want his boss to know what our plan was. We walked our horses to the other side of the dune and then we took off. It was one of the most exhilarating experiences of my life. At one point I got slightly ahead of my guide as we were galloping, and he had one of those Oh-my-God looks on his face. I slowed my horse and told the guide I had my horse under control and all was fine. It was just a fifteen-minute ride in the Sahara Desert—but oh, how glorious!

Team-Teaching Abroad

As we neared the late 1990s and the 2000s, and as more of my colleagues were teaching abroad, I began to get interested in team-teaching. It was an opportunity to travel with others and to get to know my colleagues in a fuller, more dimensional way. I team-taught with a number of different people, and eventually an agent formed a Screenwriting Summit which included my colleagues Syd Field, Michael Hauge, John Truby, myself, and later Christopher Vogler. We went to Mexico City, Toronto, Vancouver, Los Angeles, New York, and Israel.

Later there was a screenwriting seminar made up of Dara Marks, Viki King, Will Akers, and myself. We did a seminar in both London and Paris.

I discovered how kind and generous most of my colleagues were. In one instance, a participant in a seminar lit into me with a criticism of my approach to screenwriting. Chris Vogler immediately stepped in, like a knight in shining armor, and put a stop to it. He said, "This kind of criticism is the mark of an insecure person." Chris kept his focus on my attacker and didn't let up until he backed down.

As we were walking down the hallway later, I thanked him profusely for what he had done. I had rarely been saved by a knight in shining armor, and it felt really good. Chris said to me, "I was not going to let you hang out to dry."

One of my team-teaching colleagues was Kathie Fong Yonada. Several of us who team-taught with her said, "We would go to the moon to team-teach with Kathie."

Kathie was well-traveled. She was extremely observant, which is a good quality to have when teaching abroad. At one point when we were walking around Singapore, I told her, "I don't feel oppressed here, and I understood it could be an oppressive society."

Kathie pointed out, "There are three cameras on us right now—one at eleven o'clock, one at three o'clock, and one at seven o'clock. We are being closely watched." She was wise and caring and had this ability to read the situation.

I was particularly interested in our trip to Singapore because most of us who were teaching were white. Kathie is Chinese-American, and I realized how much it meant to the people in the Singapore classroom to see someone who looked like them. I know they liked both of us, but there was a special connection I observed between Kathie and the class, which opened up my eyes to how important it is to have diverse people teaching, because all of us teaching from the United States at this time were Caucasian except for Kathie.

Kathie's ability to observe and to be cautious served us well on the Singapore trip. We were supposed to go on to Jakarta, Indonesia, to do a seminar there with the same Singapore host. But Jakarta got flooded, and there was a question whether it would be safe to go. Kathie and I and our host decided we needed to reach a consensus and if one of us decided it wasn't safe, we wouldn't go. Our host in Jakarta sent us pictures and took the drive from the airport to the hotel to make sure we could get through. We reached a consensus it was safe, and it was.

Presumptions Overturned

In the late 1980s into the early 1990s there were seven men teaching abroad, and I was the only woman. I set out to equalize the playing field, and I began to recommend my female colleagues wherever I did a seminar. I realized they were not as well-known as the men, but no one seemed to resent my recommendations. It took two years to change the equation, but by the early to mid-1990s there were seven women teaching abroad, as well as seven men. After that, as more teachers came onto the scene it seemed to remain fairly equal in numbers.

When I started team-teaching, I had been teaching on my own for about ten years. I went into team-teaching seminars with presumptions that all of us were experienced as teachers and that all of us had the same professional standards. I was wrong. I learned through several situations that some colleagues didn't arrive on time or stick to their time schedules. Classes were carefully planned out, so it was important everyone end on time, but some did not.

Some of the teachers had never used a flip chart or a blackboard or a whiteboard. When we would get to low-tech situations, they were at a loss and very anxious. I did practice sessions with my colleagues writing on flip charts and turning the pages and reset up the room so the flip chart was right next to them.

Most of my colleagues used PowerPoint which I rarely did since I'd watched it fail so often. Even after doing practice sessions the day before, sometimes it didn't work the next morning. Our Israel class started forty-five minutes late due to technical issues.

Having team-taught with both men and with women, I must say the women were far more adventurous. We were the ones who would rent a car or sign up for the day trip to see some area of the country we were visiting. We were the ones to get on the horse, on the boat, on the bus. We kept saying *yes*.

Handling Danger

Some of these seminars were in potentially dangerous locations. I was invited to Russia and Kazakhstan and Nigeria and South Africa and Iraq and Iran. It could be difficult to assess whether these places were dangerous. I wasn't too concerned when I went to London or Paris because

I'd been there before or Berlin or Vienna, but I had no way to know how to make a judgment call on some of these other places. I wanted to be cautious but not close off opportunities.

My friend and colleague Pamela Jaye Smith came to my rescue. She was part of a military think tank, and she knew a number of generals and colonels. So I turned to Pamela when I wasn't sure how to assess the situation and whether to say *yes* or *no* to the invitation. I would tell her where I would be going, and she would ask the generals and colonels to give an assessment. They would give me more information than I could get from the State Department because they knew all the nuances and the details. They said that Kazakhstan was friendly to Americans and that it would be fine. Unfortunately, the seminar got canceled. They even said Nigeria would be fine because we would go to the Garden City in the south and not to Lagos in the north, but they advised that if I went, not to fly through Lagos but to take another route. That seminar was also canceled.

They questioned Kurdistan which was in northern Iraq during the Iraq war. I said *no* which was a good decision because the airport was bombed the week before I would have arrived.

They said Iran might be all right, but I would be teaching at a film festival, and if there were a controversy over a film, even though I had nothing to do with that film, I would stand out as an American, and there were enough anti-American forces that I might not be safe. I said, "No."

I did go to Dubai. I went to South Africa, and I followed all orders. My team partner on that trip had the attitude that all big cities were violent, and therefore we should just do what we want. I told her she could do what she wanted, but I was going to follow the rules. And the rules were very specific. The hotel receptionist would say, "You can walk to this restaurant, but don't walk on the street on the left; walk on the street on the right, and come back exactly that same way. You are not safe going on the street on the left, but you will be safe on the other street." I took all these hints and advices seriously.

Unpacking

I didn't really prefer team-teaching to teaching alone. Both were almost always wonderful. I did occasionally run into problems with my host. Three didn't pay me when they were supposed to, but I eventually got my money. I only got angry with a host once who was always late picking me up at the hotel—by at least an hour or two—and who was so full of himself that my patience wore very thin. He was deceptive and dishonest, and on the last day I did confront him, and he apologized.

I let my hosts know before I arrived that I liked an early dinner, and that I kept my evenings very quiet when I was teaching the next day. I made exceptions for the Spanish tuna. But there were inherent dangers, especially when traveling with someone who took chances that I would not take. When I got wind of that personality, I said *no* to team-teaching with that person.

But for somebody who wanted adventure and wanted to travel—what a life it was.

Linda's Trivia

The most interesting place I have been is Cambodia, where I didn't give a seminar but worked with writers and producers on a script. I was in Phnom Penh and Angor Watt and one of my peak experiences was singing a duet in one of the temples in Angor Watt.

Chapter Nine
Let Me Not Be Crazy About Money

There are only a few things on the list of human traits that fall under the category of "things that we really don't know what to do with." These can include religion, sex, politics, and money. There are many people who go a little nutty when trying to deal with these topics. They either think they know what to do and then run amok with their behavior, or they don't have the slightest idea what to do and throw up their hands and easily fall into the category of "stupid things I've said and done in life."

My relationship with money was probably similar to many others. You either didn't have enough and were squeezing every penny or had too much and didn't know how to be wise with it.

I started working at my father's drugstore when I was twelve and saved all the money I earned for college. During high school and college, I worked a few small jobs, including reading assignments to a blind woman and typing papers. After grad school and after my first marriage, I got several low-paying teaching jobs and just skirted by. I have no idea how I paid my rent and food at times during those years, but somehow I did. One time in graduate school when I wasn't sure how I would pay the rent that month, a drunken woman crashed into my little VW Bug at 4 a.m. just as a police car was coming around the corner. The amount she owed me for repairs was equal to rent, so my rent got paid in a most miraculous way. A friend helped me get the dent out with a toilet plunger.

I squeaked by financially from 1971 until the mid-1980s. When my business began to take off around 1984, I realized I was afraid of money and afraid what I would do if I had more than enough.

I decided I wanted to be smart about money instead of dumb, which didn't give one a whole lot to go on except a good intention. But lo and behold, shortly after I decided this, I met somebody who became very important and influential on this subject.

Marsha (not her real name) was the President of the National Organization of Women Business Owners—the Los Angeles chapter—and she took me under her wing. She dealt with insurance as well as being a financial advisor, mainly in terms of annuities and mutual funds and, to some extent, stocks and bonds.

Thus began my education.

From Rags to Some Riches

As Marsha told me, "I started working with you on money management when you had nothing but a muumuu and a pair of tennis shoes to your name." It wasn't quite that bad, but I was definitely living on the edge. And the only way I could begin my business as a script consultant was to get my expenses down so low that I could make it—even if I only had a few clients a month.

Marsha suggested that I get some insurance. She pointed out that an entrepreneur is responsible for everything. I didn't have a corporation or a company behind me. I didn't have wealthy parents. I wasn't even making enough money to put into Social Security. She set me up with a plan that would give me some money if I got ill.

Once she set me up with some basics, we began to discuss goals. My first goal was to not lose money. I realized that investments go up and down, but I didn't want to be stupid, such as trying to make fast money and investing in dubious places.

I wanted a comfortable retirement. That didn't mean having millions in the bank, but it did mean trying to set things up so when I did retire, there was money coming in.

I wanted to be able to travel and to have good advice on any major purchase. I wanted somebody who would be able to keep an eye on what was happening with my investments and let me know what I could do and what I couldn't do.

All of my trips abroad included the plane tickets, hotel accommodations, being hosted for all of my meals, and a seminar fee. But that also meant taking advantage of this wonderful opportunity to be in so many places around the world and meeting people from many different cultures. Even though I was making money, I still wanted to make sure that I had money I could spend in these locations and take vacation time.

When I started to have more income than outgo, I got a little nutty about having extra money. Both Judith and Marsha helped train me. Judith taught me to put extra money into the business until my income had stabilized. Marsha helped me plan. We invested mainly in annuities that would come due when I was around seventy.

At least once a year, Marsha and I went through everything, discussed our choices and rechecked whether we were following our intent and whether we wanted to make any changes. We went through a short period of investing in stocks, and then Marsha said that things were not going like she wanted, so we returned to mutual funds. We had discussions about socially conscious investments and made deliberate choices not to invest in war, tobacco, or firearms. Our choices also included looking at corporate policies in terms of how the workers were cared for and if there was diversity in the workforce.

And Then Came the Big Desires

Peter and I wanted to buy a home, and after we had been married a few years we bought a small bungalow in Venice, California, just a few miles from the ocean. I was teaching in New Zealand when we were finishing this purchase, and the realtor wanted to see a few thousand dollars more in our account, which was about the same amount of money that New Zealand would be paying me when I finished the job in another week. New Zealand agreed to pay me early, so we could get the house. I am always thankful to the entire country of New Zealand as well as the New Zealand Film Commission for this first big step.

Then there were the horses. In 1991 I went back to horses and started taking lessons and going on week-long horseback-riding vacations. Although the expenses were not big at the beginning, it was difficult for me to hold myself back when I found a new joy. Some of my riding vacations were in France, Spain, and Italy, as well as Monument Valley, the Pony Express Ride in Wyoming, and along the Pacific coast. Marsha approved all of these decisions.

Marsha gave me another good piece of advice when I was thinking of buying a horse: "You can take money from your fund to buy a horse, but you need to be able to make enough money every month that your income will pay for the horse lessons and room and board and the horse shows you want to do."

We began planning to move to Colorado in 2002. I saw my dream house when I was visiting the mountains near Colorado Springs the day before 9/11. Marsha and I again did an analysis to see if this move was possible. I realized when I was in Los Angeles that one of the stupidest things people do with money is to keep upgrading their house. They keep buying bigger and showier homes and become house poor. We didn't want to buy into the Hollywood culture that looks for externals to prove that we were doing well. We also realized that a new house could be a temptation rather than a blessing. I had to consider whether moving would ruin my script-consulting business. Peter had to consider whether he could restart his massage and acupuncture business in Colorado. After planning and pondering, we bought our dream house December 23, 2001.

The house was almost one hundred years old. It was made of beautiful big logs and sat on 1.68 acres of land. It included a separate cabin for my office. Thousands of pine trees were within our view. From our bathroom window we could see a Ferris wheel at the North Pole—a tourist place across the road where Santa lived. It was five miles from Colorado Springs but right in the mountains—not even on the edge or in the foothills—in the mountains! And it cost two thirds of what we received for our little bungalow in Venice which was on much less land and had half the square footage of our new home.

Marsha gave us another piece of advice. She said, "When you move, I want you to have $50,000 in a savings account because something is going to come up when you arrive. That might mean there's an electrical problem or you need to repaint or something needs to be changed in the plumbing or there's something that might need to be remodeled that you had not thought of. I don't want you to do this move with stress. Many people put all their money into buying the house and don't leave any for what might need to be done after the move."

And of course, there were some things—like installing a hardwood floor in the cabin and putting a railing and stairs on the side of the hill that went down to the cabin office. We didn't want to think of ourselves as Jack and Jill rolling down the hill every morning to work.

From Horses to Pianos

I bought my first horse in 2003 and had a horse until 2013. After my horse stage, it was the piano that kept calling to me. By this time, I had changed financial advisors because Marsha was retiring, and I found a wonderful person in Colorado Springs. Now Jeff began to get the questions: "Jeff, can I buy a grand piano?"

"Yes, if it's under $50,000 which means you can't buy the $66,000 Steinway or the $150,000 Bosendorfer."

That was fine because I fell in love with the Estonia 5'6" grand piano, which was less expensive.

Then I started doing two-piano work and got permission to buy the five-foot Yamaha Baby Grand. The two pianos nestled next to each other and were very fond of each other.

When I retired in 2020 everything worked out just as it had been planned in the 1980s.

I'm doing just fine.

Unpacking

During these years I could see how many decisions needed to be made about money. I watched friends make decisions around money—some of them not too smart. Others did something similar to what we had done. We were able to buy a house, take some big trips, and have a fairly stable life due to some very good financial advice.

One of my favorite quotes comes from the play and film *Hello Dolly*: "Money, pardon the expression, is like manure. It's not worth a thing unless it's spread around, encouraging young things to grow." Money helped me grow—and stay smart.

Linda's Trivia

Besides the horses and pianos, my favorite expensive purchase is a pair of embroidered boots I bought in Las Vegas in 1986 for $250.00. I still wear them, but it seemed like a crazy thing to do. It was the first time in years I could splurge.

Chapter Ten
Famous People I Met or Was in the Presence Of

Working in the film industry includes those occasional moments of meeting famous people or being around them and being a bit gobsmacked. Since I worked with screenwriters who were generally unknown to the public, I only occasionally met more public figures, such as actors or directors or producers.

Here are some of the more interesting interactions and meetings I have had over the years.

Ron Howard

When I was writing my book on *The Collaborative Art of Filmmaking* with Dr. Edward J. Whetmore, we set out to interview some of the biggest names in Hollywood who were known in each of the important areas in filmmaking. These included directors and actors and screenwriters and directors of photography and editors. We were surprised that seventy people said *yes* to an interview. Our book was not an interview book. It was more of a book that helped the reader understand the different aspects of these various art forms through quotes from these famous people. These were integrated as they explained how a film was put together and how these artists worked collaboratively.

Ron Howard was on our list, and I left a message with his secretary, wondering if there was a chance of interviewing him. About a day later I received a phone call and this male voice said, "This is Ron Howard." After I took a deep breath and a bit of a gulp, I asked him if I could interview him, and he asked me how much time I would like. I mentioned that if I could get ten to twenty minutes, even over the phone, that would be great. He said, "Why don't you come to my office, and we'll have lunch, and I'll give you two hours." He made sure to get my order for Chinese food (cashew chicken—how could I forget that?). It turned out that his father had given him a copy of my book *Making a Good Script Great* shortly after it came out, so both he and his partner at Imagine Productions—producer Brian Grazer—knew who I was and seemed interested in the book.

Ron was forthcoming about why he became a director. He said, "The director gets to play with everyone." He talked to me about the importance of the collaborative process and how he had become more collaborative over the years as he recognized he was working with some of the greatest people in these various areas that are needed for a great film. He said, "It would be stupid of me to have all this valuable knowledge and not be using the remarkable contributions that each of these people can give to make a great film."

After the interview, I had his secretary's email, and when I needed to ask a question, I would email her and would get a reply, usually that same day. When I was writing my book *Spiritual Steps on the Road to Success* in 2008, I remembered that somebody told me they thought Ron was a Presbyterian, and I thought he might be an interesting interview since I was trying to get well-rounded quotes on the relationship between success and spirituality. Ron called me to reply to this request on Caucus Day in Colorado. I was the precinct chair for our area, which is just outside of Colorado Springs in the mountains, and mentioned that to him and that the caucus would be that evening. Our conversation quickly turned to politics. Ron was fascinated with how a caucus worked. We were both Democrats, and he was a huge Hillary Clinton supporter. I mentioned that my husband and I liked both Clinton and Obama and that we had decided one of us would vote for Hillary and one for Obama. Peter voted for Hillary, and I voted for Obama.

Ron explained to me that he was not the best person for an interview for that book, but he remained somewhat accessible to me, and his secretary always responded. Sometimes I just had research questions for Ron and sometimes just wanted to send him a note about how much I liked his last film.

A number of people who knew I had interviewed Ron jumped to the conclusion that we had a close personal relationship and I could call him to help sell the writer's script. That was not the relationship. There was only one time I mentioned a script I had worked on to the secretary to see if Ron might be interested because I thought it would be a good match. It was clear to me that I had crossed a boundary and that this relationship did not put me in a position to recommend scripts. It was professional and respectful and my interchanges were to be about the book.

Raquel Welch

What do you say to Raquel Welch when you're introduced to her at a Television Academy reception? Well, you have to think fast because clearly this was not going to be a long conversation. I said what I thought might be a bit stupid but turned out to be a really good idea: "How do you manage to stay so beautiful year after year?"

She mentioned that she went to the gym often, which seemed to be the extent of our interchange. But a half-hour later, when she spoke to the Television Academy, she mentioned that someone (me) she'd talked to at the reception had asked that question, so obviously it meant something to her. I think it was a very good thing to say.

Rob O'Neill

You may not have heard of this person, but you certainly have heard about what he did. He was the person who shot Osama bin Laden and was the head of the Navy Seal team that went into that compound. The movie *Zero Dark Thirty* was partly about this team, although they did not identify specific people.

I was in Nashville to give a seminar and a few speeches. One of my clients who was a screenwriter was also a public relations person, and Rob was her client. Paula had arranged for me to be shown around Nashville by a friend of hers and then invited me for a private tour of the Gibson guitar factory, which she was giving for Rob and a few of his friends. I, of course, said *yes* and expected him to be a very burly, perhaps even coarse, person who may have had a heavy load on his shoulders. Was I ever wrong! He was one of the classiest and good-natured people I had ever met. Since we were a small group of about seven people, it turned out that as we did this ninety-minute tour, Rob and I often walked through the hallways together from section to section of the factory. We had time to chat a bit, and he mentioned that when they were in the helicopter going to the compound, one of his team said, "What is the worst-case scenario for what we are about to do?" Rob replied, somewhat jokingly, "We could lose one of the two helicopters." And they did.

Two Really Gorgeous Men—Tom Selleck and Screenwriter Ernest Thompson

There is a reason that some people become real stars. They have a presence, and it creates waves that go out to anybody near them or anyone watching them. In the 1990s, I had the qualifications to join the Academy of Television Arts and Sciences—the group that puts on the Emmy Awards and has many thousands of members in various categories such as actors and directors and producers.

The Academy had a number of receptions as well as weekends where we watched television movies and miniseries and series nominated for Emmys and then voted on which should be the winner. At one of these receptions, I was standing in the hallway and looked up and saw Tom Selleck about eight feet away from me talking to somebody. He was gorgeous and classy and seemed soft-spoken and considerate. I later learned that my friend Mara Purl used to date him, and I couldn't figure out how anyone could have dinner or a date with someone like that or even try to talk to this person and keep one's mind on anything that was being said. I guess there are some people who can be in the midst of this gorgeousness and keep their wits about them. It is clear I was not one of these people.

The other most gorgeous man I met was screenwriter Ernest Thompson who won an Academy Award for best screenwriting for *On Golden Pond*.

Laura, one of my colleagues, invited me to give a seminar in Boston and to speak at Boston College. When we went to the Green Room at the college where we waited to go to the class, I was introduced to Ernest Thompson, who was speaking in another class. He fit in the category often used to describe very attractive male characters in screenplays: "ruggedly handsome." I would add "amazingly classy" because of the way he dressed. He had on khakis and beautiful shoes and a bomber jacket and a white shirt and, I think, a white silk scarf. As we walked down the hallway to our individual classes, I was so dumbstruck by his looks that I couldn't say a word—which is highly unusual for me because I tend to be very extroverted and talkative. Laura, who was five months pregnant, was chattering away. We came to a parting of the ways as he went in one direction to his class, and Laura and I went in another direction to the class where

I would be speaking. As we left, we looked at each other and sank into the protection of a bench that just happened to be there in the hallway. I asked, "How were you able to talk in the middle of that gorgeousness?"

And Laura replied, "I have never seen anyone that gorgeous, and all I could do was chatter away."

I explained, "I have never seen anyone that gorgeous, so I became speechless, which I have never done."

I later learned that Kayleigh, a friend of mine who lives a mile down the road from our house in Colorado, used to date Ernest. So I guess I am one degree of separation, not just from having been near these men, but from the women they used to date.

Dr. Shri Nehru—Ambassador to the United Nations and Cousin to Prime Minister Nehru

Growing up in a small town seemed as if not much of interest was going to happen to me in my early years. But it turns out my mother was much like the person I became, saying *yes* to opportunities.

My mother met a woman who lived near Milwaukee and who mentioned that she was friends with Dr. Nehru. He was going to be coming to the United States and would love to see more of the country than just the big cities. Mother immediately invited the Nehrus—through this woman—to come to Peshtigo. She would arrange a tour of the factories we had in Peshtigo for them, which included a paper mill, a boat factory, and Unit Structures, which built the big arches that formed the frames of new buildings.

Mother was also going to give a piano concert and a reception for them. She tried to teach my sister and me that the correct response when meeting such a distinguished person was to say, "Very pleased to meet you." She had us practice this—but when we met the Nehrus, I said the appropriate words since I'd learned my dialogue well, and Holly said, "Hi."

Dr. Nehru and his wife were lovely, kind people. They stayed at our home in the master bedroom, and Holly and I stayed with friends. But we did get to go to the reception. As they were ready to leave our home after several days, Mother asked them if there was something in our house they would like to take home as a gift. They were Hindu, but they chose a little ceramic figurine of The Lord's Prayer.

Several years later, the Nehrus invited Mom and Dad to New York for a private tour of the United Nations. And when I was in high school, the woman who had originally made this introduction invited us to her home near Milwaukee because the Nehrus would be there. They had two grand pianos in their home, and Mom and Holly and I did a concert, which included vocal and piano duets and two-piano work. They were two of the loveliest people I had ever met. It surprised me that even in little Peshtigo these experiences could happen.

Other Famous Encounters

I grew up watching the *Lorreta Young Show* every week and remembering her wise sayings and beautiful dresses. During my time in Los Angeles, she was being honored by Women in Film and being given their Crystal Award. Since I was a member, I managed to get a message to her to ask if I could meet her briefly to thank her for her influence on me. She said *yes*, and I had a moment where I gave her my book. She later sent me a spiritual book as a thank you. When I was writing my book *When Women Call the Shots*, I asked if I could interview her, and she invited me to her home. I had no idea she had started in the film business as a little girl and had such an impact in television and film. Her intention with her television series was to speak to girls—and that she did with me.

Interviewing a number of famous people showed me that sometimes there was that spark with them that made it friendly and warm and not just a matter of good information. I felt that spark when I interviewed Liv Ullman in Sweden. I sat across from her looking into those grey eyes and felt she liked me as I liked her. I also felt that spark when I interviewed Mary McDonald from *Dances with Wolves*, and when I interviewed the famous actor and acting teacher Nina Foch. When I left the interview with Nina, I mistakenly left my tape recorder behind. I called her a few hours later so I could pick it up, and she said her son had called and asked her what she had done today. She told him she had been interviewed by me, and the son said, "You mean Linda Seger was at your house talking to you?" He was impressed.

Unpacking

I began to learn that the interview subject often enjoyed the interview as much as I did. I took for granted that they had very little time and I should get the interview over with as soon as possible. I learned instead to try and gage whether the person was willing to give me more time and to ask them for another ten minutes. When I talked to Ron Howard about the Colorado Caucus, I think he would have loved to talk with me further to get an insider's view on how politics worked in Colorado.

When I finished my interview with Loretta Young, she took one of her scrapbooks out for us to look at together, then she quickly put it back on the table and said, "You wouldn't be interested in that." Of course I would, but I didn't have the wherewithal to think quickly and tell her how much I would enjoy doing that with her. Instead, we ended on a friendly note, and I missed out on another special opportunity.

Linda's Triva

Favorite comment from a famous person: I met Robert Rodat, the screenwriter of *Saving Private Ryan*. Clearly, he knew my work and said to me: "How does it feel seeing your work on the screen?" I was dumbstruck.

Chapter Eleven
Famous People Who Said Bad Things About Me

Let's start with Warren Beatty. I had a part-time assistant who had some interaction with him. He mentioned to her that he was struggling with a script. She suggested that he hire me because my business was about "identifying, analyzing, and helping solve difficult script problems."

He clearly had heard of me and told my assistant, "What good is she anyway? Has she ever won an Academy Award?"

My assistant answered him, "No, but she's really good at what she does."

This was the main criticism people had about me, mainly from people who didn't know me. They couldn't understand how I could be a good script consultant if I weren't a screenwriter. This criticism came from all corners and disappeared when I worked with somebody.

Another assistant was applying for a job with the producer Don Simpson, who was part of the Simpson-Bruckheimer team, who produced such hits as *Top Gun*, *Flashdance*, and *Pirates of the Caribbean*. As he walked her to the car after the interview, he noticed that she had my book *Making a Good Script Great* on the passenger seat. He made a snide comment to her about the book. My assistant looked at him and said, "I'm out of here!" She left.

I said to her, "Obviously you didn't get the job."

She replied, "I wouldn't want a job with somebody that spoke badly about you."

Oh, I loved my assistants! They were great workers for me and wonderful people.

My Favorite Bad Comment Because It Was Such a Whopper

In the early 1990s, I was invited to do a seminar in Australia at the Australian Film and Television School. It was going to be a seminar, team-taught with Frank Pierson, the Academy-Award-winning writer who had written *Dog Day Afternoon* and several other well-known screenwriters.

The Writers Guild of Australia, at the same time, was doing a seminar with the writer Hanif Kareishi, who had written *My Beautiful Launderette* which was a huge hit. The film school decided that it would be wonderful for the people in my class to hear Hanif speak during the noon hour.

The head of the film school was one of my favorite hosts—Paul Thompson. As he interviewed Hanif, he solicited questions from the audience. One of the audience members raised his hand and asked Hanif the question: "What do you think of people like Syd Field and Linda Seger?" This audience member knew very well that I was sitting in the audience, but Hanif clearly did not know that. And why would he? We were in Australia after all. We were thousands of miles away from our homes.

Hanif went into the question full throttle. He clearly had an opinion about people like us. He said, "These people are creatively dead. Run away from them as fast as you can."

Well! It seemed everyone took a deep breath, and I wondered if there was something I should say. I quickly realized I did not have to say anything. All I had to do was wait and see what would happen next.

At that moment, Paul gently turned to Hanif and said, "Linda Seger is teaching at our school this week, and she's in this audience." I couldn't see Hanif from my seat, but Paul later told me that he had never seen anyone turn so many different colors—red and yellow and green and blue.

Within seconds, the first hand went up and the audience member said, "I'm taking the class from Linda now, and it is one of the best classes I've ever taken."

The next hand went up; "I really love Linda's book *Making a Good Script Great*, and it has really helped with my writing."

The next hand went up with a similar sentiment. There were four or five hands in my defense. I knew that Paul would make sure those people were heard because he was the one who had invited me and had great respect for me just as I had for him.

People on the Train and the Trail

After I had been doing my work for some years, I became known—not only to people who had met me, but to people who had heard about me. Many times, they didn't understand what I did but nevertheless had an attitude about me, some of them positive and some of them negative.

Many of them had misinformation, which would get me upset or irritate me as I tried to figure out what to do. My dear and wise friend Cathleen said to me, "If you're going to be a public figure, you're going to have to accept that people will say things that have no basis in fact. And there's nothing you can do about it. Otherwise, don't be a public figure."

I also realized that when we start putting ourselves out in public, we are often once removed from people who actually know us. They might know someone who consulted with me or took a seminar from me and formed an opinion about me. They then tell others about me and then others tell others as well.

Opinions of me would pop up in the most random places. Friends would sometimes recount to me stories of when they were hiking and met somebody who was writing a screenplay. They would mention that they knew me, and the other person sometimes replied, "How could she help somebody with their screenplay when she's not a screenwriter?" Stories were recounted to me of the same thing happening to people a friend talked to on a train or at an airport.

Sometimes personal questions came up. People wondered what I was like. They wanted to "get the skinny" on me. One friend in our Santa Monica Friends Meeting (Quakers) said to me, "Are you kind of a star?"

I answered, "I am, in my field."

She responded, "I was talking to somebody who was writing a screenplay, and I mentioned you, and she suddenly wanted to know all sorts of things about you."

I said to her, "What did you say?"

She replied, "I told her you were very nice." I told her that was the correct response.

I recounted the story to a friend. About a week later he was on a train, and the subject came up again. Johnny remembered what I had told him—the correct reply is, "She is very nice."

Bad Things I Said About Others

I soon learned word gets around quickly when you are famous and you say bad—or good—things. After I moved to Colorado, I went back to Los Angeles to do a seminar. During the break I went into the gift store, and when I bought something, I was astounded at the high city tax that was added to the price. I said something to the sales woman that must have had a bit of a sharp edge to it. It wasn't her fault that there was this high tax, but I guess my amazement was rather reactive and should not have fallen on her. One of the students in my class observed this interaction and then wrote about it on the internet, letting everybody know I was not so nice.

People have opinions—some of them good and some of them bad. The only control we have is over our own behavior, and everything else has to be let go.

I developed a policy I would never speak badly about a colleague in public. On the other hand, sometimes colleagues do disgusting things, and there were times I needed to talk about these things and let somebody know how I felt. I wanted to be honest about my feelings and opinions, but they were not for public consumption. If I had to be catty about somebody, I called my wise and discrete friend, film mythologist Pamela Jaye Smith. I would tell Pamela, "I just need to be catty about something a colleague just did, but I can't let this get out into public." Pamela would say, "Meow, do tell."

Don't Say Bad Things— Even in Copenhagen

I stuck to my policy of not saying bad things about a colleague, but I broke my policy once during a seminar in Copenhagen. The film *Age of Innocence* had come out that year, and I found it overly sentimental and cloying, including the title sequence which had lots of lace and doilies. I didn't know that the title sequence was done by a very famous person who had done titles for Alfred Hitchcock films and had pioneered a new way of doing titles. His name was Saul Bass. He was highly respected, but I didn't know that. I figured in Copenhagen I was safe to give a snide comment about the film and titles. So, I compromised my policy and let the class know what I thought.

That evening, I was going out to dinner with a student and saw another student from my class in the hotel lobby. I thought she might be going to dinner with us. She said, "I'm meeting Saul Bass for dinner, who is here in the same hotel and sponsored by another organization." My heart sank and I hoped she was a nicer person than me. She said, "Would you like to meet him?" I said, "Yes."

She introduced us as he got out of the elevator, and I said, "I'm very pleased to meet you. I'm familiar with your work."

That taught me a lesson. Even when far away in a foreign land, stick to the policy.

Unpacking

Eventually it became clear to me that those of us who become public figures have a responsibility. We have the potential to be role models and to lift people up as we discuss our fields of expertise rather than to use the opportunity to tear them down. This Saul Bass episode taught me such a valuable lesson as I did some research on him and felt ashamed for how I had acted.

Linda's Trivia

A great compliment I got from a famous person came from Ron Howard. He gave me an endorsement for my book *Making a Good Script Great* that said, "I have used Linda's book on every movie starting with *Apollo 13*." It's nice to feel useful.

Chapter Twelve
My Magnificent Chapter— The Horses

By the late 1980s, I was doing quite well. I had a good steady stream of clients. My first book, *Making a Good Script Great*, was published at the end of 1987. I had already given seminars around the United States and was starting to do seminars abroad.

Even a little bit of fame starts building a bubble of protection. Suddenly there are enough people out there who think you are Wonderful and The Very Best. There are interviews and articles written and endorsements. There was the occasional, "Oh my God. Is that Linda Seger!" My friend Cathleen would remind me, "Remember. Visions of you have not been seen in Bolivia!"

The Bubble protects any vulnerabilities. It reinforces the idea of being tremendous, confident, really good at what you do, and very knowledgeable. And it protects you. Others don't know that you get nervous at times, and that you realize in the middle of the seminar that you aren't doing a good job, or you get jealous of your colleagues, and are sometimes unsure of yourself.

The Bubble gives you special privileges. When you're a little bit famous, the paths do part at times. I've had private tours of cathedrals after hours because my host explained to the guard who I was. There's the occasional limo ride and the front-row tickets to a cultural event. It's easy to start believing The Press and the Endorsers and live in this comfortable, successful, appreciated position. It's a wonderful place to be—and I realized it was a dangerous place to be.

The Bubble cuts you off from the rest of the world. I discovered I was able to control my environment quite well and choose where I went and who I associated with and, of course, I gravitated to those who reinforced the good things being said about me. The Bubble doesn't allow you to engage and interact with the negative forces—whether that means people who are critical or people who are not in the same privileged position as you. From a purely social-justice viewpoint, it seemed like a faulty idea to protect myself from the struggles and difficulties that I had once gone through and that many people might be currently going through. Being so privileged and Above-it-All also seemed to cut me off from the potential of transformational experiences.

So what did I do about this? I went back to horseback riding.

Horses Changed My Life

I had liked horses since the first time I saw one when I was four. I occasionally rode a Shetland pony, Penny, in grade school and high school, and I took riding lessons in my early twenties. In 1988, when I was in my early forties, I saw an article about a dude ranch where they took clients on a cattle drive. I saved the article and thought it would be wonderful to actually drive cattle—especially since my favorite Western in the 1950s was *Rawhide* where they drove cattle all the time.

I did nothing about this spark of a desire until after I saw *City Slickers*. That movie changed my life. I realized that I would regret not following through on something that seemed to be calling to me. I was not naturally an athletic person nor confident in my physical ability. And I hadn't been on a horse for about twenty years, but I knew that if I did not do this now in my forties, this would not be something I could do in my fifties or sixties. I found the article and signed up for the cattle drive for the end of May the following year.

This began a twenty-two-year passion. I knew I would need to go into training to do this cattle drive because it meant being in the saddle for five to eight hours a day. I would need to know what kind of riding we would be doing. Would we need to jump a log? Wade through a river? Gallop up a hill? Would the cows get away from us? I had just received a royalty check and decided to use it toward riding lessons. I joined the Malibu Riding and Tennis Club (where

Robert Redford and Dustin Hoffman were members) and began to take lessons and increase the time of trail rides from one hour to four hours at a time.

The world of horses began to burst my Bubble. When I took lessons, I was a beginner or early intermediate rider. I was never the best of the bunch. I didn't know very much about caring for a horse. And nobody was going to say I was wonderful and amazing based on my ability. No one really cared that I had written two books. What did count on the cattle drive was whether I could get the cows out of the thicket and keep them going forward.

I loved riding slowly through the canyons with the six hundred cows. I liked camping out—which surprised me since I had done so little of it. I liked having very little—my jeans and boots and a few T-shirts. I loved the experience of getting to meet people who were in such different fields than I was and had such different lives than I had. Two of my favorite people on the ride were a truck driver and a man who worked at a factory in Ohio.

One of the riders told me that there were riding vacations all over the world, and he gave me the name of the company. This began twelve years of taking one-week riding vacations—to dude ranches, to Provence and Camargue in France, to the countryside of Italy, from hacienda to hacienda in Spain. I even did the Pony Express ride, which included a twenty-minute gallop of five miles. We also rode in the beauty of Monument Valley and along the coast of Mendocino in northern California.

I received one of my first and very few compliments about my horseback riding on the Mendocino trip. One of the women on the trip confessed to me on Tuesday, the second day riding, that she had lied on her application form and said she was a very good horseback rider. She admitted to me she had never been on a horse and realized she was in way, way over her head. She had a natural athletic ability and physical courage because she was a yoga teacher, but she admitted that the first gallop told her she had better figure something out fast.

She did. She said to me, "I realized I was in deep shit. I looked around at the twenty-two riders in our group and looked for the person who seemed the most confident and knowledgeable and knew what she was doing. That was you. I got in the line right behind you and did everything you did." This woman was flying by the end of the week and having the time of her life.

It's Time to Buy a Horse

When we moved to Colorado in 2002, I began seriously considering getting a horse.

I found a terrific teacher, and with her help we started looking for a horse. This, of course, meant I also had to get a truck and a horse trailer because I wanted to enter horse shows as well as continue to do trail rides.

So I bought my first horse, Coastin' Abigail Sue—Abby for short. She was a beautiful Paint who was wonderful and frustrating. Thankfully I had teachers who could show me what to do because I knew nothing about owning a horse.

Preparing for Horse Shows

Since I was rarely without new ideas—some of which were expensive—I got interested in a form of Western horseback riding called reining. This included competitions where you rode to music in costume and integrated difficult moves into the choreography. The competitions were something like ice-skating competitions. We had four minutes to perform and were disqualified if we went over four minutes. We had seven different moves to integrate into the choreography, and we were graded on technique and artistry. My artistry was better than my technique.

Reining is considered the most difficult form of Western riding because of the difficulties of the maneuvers. It is based on the moves the horse makes when moving cows. Sometimes the horse has to make a sudden stop and swirl around on his back feet and go in another direction. That move got integrated into reining.

Reining also grew out of the respect ranchers had for each other and the support they gave each other. In this competition, the competitors tended to be very supportive of each other. Trainers encouraged other horse riders, even when they hardly knew the person. Around my sixth year of doing reining, a trainer came up after my ride and told me how much I had improved. I had never seen this man before and asked him if he had been watching me. He said, "I have watched you for the last six years, and you and your horse are very happy. You started out looking like a monkey on horseback, but you look really good now." Judges told me, "You look like you're having fun."

The horse had to be trained in the maneuvers and the rider had to be trained to give the correct cue. Some of the maneuvers included spins, where the horse spins around in a circle on its back feet. The horse had to do a backup and flying lead changes when moving from a circle to the left to doing a circle to the right. He had to skip a beat in the middle of the circle to get his feet in the right position as he changed direction. This took a very specific cue from the rider, which took me about five years to learn. The horse also did sliding stops, which meant you galloped as fast as you could in the arena and brought the horse to a rapid stop, so his feet slid through the sand as he came to an abrupt halt. Great riders might do a slide of thirty feet or more. Most of mine were five-feet long, but I once did one that was fifteen-feet long.

All of this means the horse has to stay in training, and the rider has to continue training. I wasn't very good at reining, but one judge did say: "If we gave a first prize for smiles, Linda would get it. However, she's getting fourth place."

Unpacking

I learned an important lesson from all of this horseback riding. We easily believe that we have to be really good at something in order to contribute. But I learned that my attitude was making a difference with other people because I was so happy when I rode in the horse shows. One rider said to me, "You help us remember what this is supposed to be about; we're supposed to have fun."

That absolutely wonderful stage of my life lasted until 2013. During that time, I had four different horses. Sometimes they got hurt and required months of rehabilitation. One of my horses got injured and could no longer do reining, so I had to give him away. I gave him to a nine-year-old, and the horse changed her life. She became a better student in school and a much more confident person because the horse brought out the best in her.

Linda's Trivia

My favorite horse of the four was Shane, who was named after my favorite Western. One of my greatest compliments came when I was in a horse show with some really top riders. A friend of mine who knew horses well said to me, "You and your horse were the only happy horses in that arena. The others were being jerked around. They were swishing their tails and putting their ears back, but you and Shane were such a good pair."

Part Three:
Crisis Points

Chapter Thirteen
But How Do I Get Off the Mountain?

I know there are people who like to live on the edge, take risks, and feel what happens when the adrenaline gushes. I am not one of those people. I rarely get myself into difficult situations. I err on the side of caution. I am open to new experiences but do things that seem reasonably safe. The few times I have been in situations that are risky and difficult and took a number of decisions to get out of them, I learned that I was sensible. I was fairly good at figuring things out even when all choices seemed to be closed doors, and I was fairly quick at figuring out when it was time to think to myself, "The person I'm with is nuts, and it's time for me to take over."

Going Hiking

In the summer of 1972, I worked at a children's camp in the hills near Marysville, California. I taught creative drama for the summer—putting on little plays daily—while also participating in campfire songs and feeding the animals and keeping a cabin full of twelve-year-olds relatively happy.

Each camp counselor had a day off every other week, and although there was not much to do in that area, I had a car and usually went off exploring with another counselor. One of the owners of the ranch was nervous about girls going off and hiking, although she seemed to have no trouble with the guys doing that on their day off. We had various attitudes about these limits, including not telling her or just saying we were going to go for a walk instead of a hike or just doing what we wanted once we got in the car.

One of the other counselors, Gail, was a hiker and told me there were these beautiful falls nearby. She bragged about having been to Outward Bound, which I knew was one of those wilderness programs, and I figured she knew what she was doing in the wilderness. Since I didn't do a lot of hiking, I presumed she would be able to identify trails, knowing which ones were the best and the safest. Wrong!

As we started the hike, I put my car keys inside my little backpack, presuming that when the time came, one of us would know how to backtrack and get us back to the car.

We started on a downhill trail because the falls were supposedly slightly below us. As we were hiking, we were somewhat surprised and perhaps even a little relieved to see there was a tent near one of the streams. This confirmed for us that we were not too isolated and that we should keep going, as we didn't want to interfere with this person's private space.

We saw the falls some hundreds of feet below us. Gail led the way along the ledge on the one side of the falls. Personally, I don't like ledges and precipices, but I trusted Gail and figured all would be fine. After all she had been to Outward Bound and knew the wilderness. Wrong.

We started down the rock that was above the falls. There was a little scrub bush to the right and a small ledge slightly to the left where we could stand and then another little ledge that was leading down the hill toward the falls.

Gail went first and held the scrubby bush with one hand, and turned around to get her feet in the right place on the ledge. I took the scrubby bush in my right hand and left hand, but the bush started to come loose. She put out her hand, so I had to make a choice—give Gail my hand or trust the scrubby bush. I decided to trust her hand which was the right decision. Just then the bush came out of the ground. Gail was holding my hand and kept screaming at me, "Dig In! Dig in!" Which I did. She managed to pull me on to the ledge. I looked back and realized we could not return that way because the scrubby brush was gone. To the right beneath us was a waterfall. To the left was a big boulder covered with moss. We were standing on a small ledge that was about three feet by two feet. Directly in front of us was a little hill that dropped at an angle for about four feet, then another little ledge, followed by the long downhill of the mountain, which did not have any other stopping places. But that was the only way down.

There did not appear to be many choices for getting down the mountain.

Gail started evaluating this big boulder. To me it looked like a no brainer. There was no way we could climb on it because it was covered in moss. That's not how Gail saw it. She said, "Maybe we could climb over that boulder." At that moment I realized I should not trust her.

Then Gail looked down the hill. She figured the second ledge would stop us. She suggested that I go first. I said, "No, I'm not sure this is going to work because I don't think that ledge is big enough to stop us. Since you think it is, you go first and catch me when I go."

"Okay," she said, rather blithely.

She started doing her little run down the first part of the hill, but the next ledge did not stop her. Then she started rolling and she rolled and she rolled and she rolled down the entire mountain—out of sight. I kept calling her name and did not hear a response. I figured she was either badly hurt or dead.

I felt the need to do something, and the choices were extremely limited at this point. There was only one way down, and it was the way Gail had gone. I needed to make some kind of decision, so I decided to test and see if the backpack would stop at the ledge. I took off my backpack and rolled it down the little hill, expecting it to stop. It didn't. It rolled and rolled and rolled down the entire mountain following Gail's path.

There was still no word from Gail. I started to assess the situation. Was there any way I could get down the ledge without rolling down the entire hill? I saw a tree to my left by the ledge, and I figured if I could roll to the left, the tree would stop me. Once I was stopped, I figured I could find my way down that hill. Just as I was trying to get up the courage to do this, Gail called out. She was at the bottom of the hill, and she said she had hurt her ankle and knee. I asked if she could come up and catch me and help me down, and she said she couldn't. I decided the only thing I could do was to follow my plan.

I'm sure if I had been a math major, I would've figured out the hypotenuse and the best angle so I would hit the tree. But since I was not a math major, the only thing I could do was to just go for it at an angle. It worked. I hit the tree, but not too hard. Then I continued slowly making my way down to where Gail was.

My backpack had followed Gail and almost hit her. I arrived where she was with the backpack nearby. So now we had other decisions. I told Gail that I had to get her back to the car without any detours and without hurting her ankle further. We remembered seeing the hiker, and I suggested we go back that route, and if he were there, he probably knew the shortest route back to the car. If he wasn't there and her ankle was really bothering her, I could leave her there and go for help, presuming he was a nice-enough guy. I told her not to take off her boot because it would make it worse for her to be walking around barefoot. I figured her foot was so swollen that she wouldn't be able to get the boot back on.

I went to my backpack to get out my car keys. They were not there. The backpack was slightly open, and the car keys had fallen out somewhere along this roll down the hill. I knew the car keys had to be on the path that Gail and the backpack had gone down, but there were many leaves and branches and grass. I had no choice except to climb up the hill on that path, hoping to see them. I started praying that I would find those car keys. Shortly after I started the prayer, I saw a leaf, and my intuition told me to look under it. I picked it up, and underneath the leaf were the car keys. So that problem was solved. Thank God!

We figured the best way to get Gail back toward the hiker's camp would be for me to boost her up onto the rocks and take the shortest route. I sometimes had to walk around because I couldn't get up on the rock without some help. Slowly we made our way to this man's camp. Near his camp there was a creek, and I suggested she soak her foot while I went over and saw if he was by his tent.

He was there. He was sitting on a rock with his shirt off. The book he was reading was lowered and well placed because it was clear to me, he was naked. I calmly explained the situation and said my friend was around the corner. He kept his book firmly in place. I turned my back. He slipped around the back of the rock, put some shorts on, got a little medical kit, and followed me around the corner.

He saw Gail and said, "Gail."

Gail saw him and said, "Ron."

You never know who you might meet in the wilderness. Ron had taught creative drama the year before at the camp where I was teaching now. He had stopped by the camp at a time I wasn't there and met Gail. Ron led us on the easiest way back to the car with Gail limping but doing okay.

The Aftermath

Just when you think it's safe and all has been resolved, stories often take an unpredictable turn. I expected to be welcomed back with a celebration dinner. I hoped to find out there was nothing seriously wrong with Gail. Perhaps we would get a hug from somebody. Wrong again.

As we were driving back, Gail began to be concerned that our hiking had led us into danger, which might cause the owner to forbid any of us to hike. So Gail asked me not to talk about it because Joy, the owner, did not want us to be hiking, specifically because of these kinds of dangers. Gail said she would explain she sprained her ankle and not say too much about what we had done and where we were.

That seemed to work okay with Gail. She was taken to the doctor the next day. She had a sprained ankle and had also hurt her knee and would later need to have surgery. There was a certain amount of fussing over Gail with a few questions asked, but on the whole, neither of us said much about the incident.

On the other hand, I had quite a few scratches and bruises. I was sore. I felt the experience was quite traumatic. But I also felt I couldn't say much. Others saw me as a bystander without realizing how many decisions I had to make to get us out of this situation.

I was really struggling with what had happened. I'm the kind of person that needs to talk it through and get feedback and have a good therapist or at least a good friend help me figure out what was going on. But there was no one to talk to, nor was there any way for me to get salve for the cuts or any help, even though my physical problems were not very serious.

I knew the camp had an infirmary with a bathtub. I asked the owner if I could take a bath and nurture myself, and she asked, "Why?" I had told her that I had been with Gail and it was somewhat scary, and she had somehow never put that together. She said *no* to my request. I then went and talked to her husband who was co-owner of the ranch. He was quite empathetic and recognized that when there were two people, they were dealing with two different kinds of traumas. One might say that our lives were not in danger, but if you saw the waterfall and the ledge and the precipice, you might change your mind about the problem. Clearly there was great peril.

Unpacking

We got through the last few weeks of the summer. But I felt traumatized by this event. I made a decision for the future and decided that when I was in the wilderness it's best not to totally rely on anyone—no matter how experienced they are. You also have to recognize that the most experienced person might be hurt, and that means that you are left to figure something out that you know nothing about. It does help to keep your wits about you and carefully assess the situation.

I also learned that after any kind of trauma I needed to talk it through and unpack the situation. I needed empathy, and I needed self-care. And I didn't get any of those at the camp even when asking for them. I figured this might be the end of these close calls, but I was wrong. There was an even closer call that was going to come some years later.

Linda's Trivia

Even before this incident, I was not fond of heights, nor of ledges and precipices. Now we plan our driving so we don't go over high mountain passes.

Chapter Fourteen
Saving a Life Isn't All It's Cracked Up to Be

Since the time I was in grade school, I've always found stories about courage and saving a life profound. There is a verse in the Bible that I read when I was at Bible camp, perhaps when I was seven or eight, that says, "Greater love hath no man than this, that a man lay down his life for his friends" (John 15:13 KJV). That verse has always had an impact on me.

When I was a young adult, I learned that a guy in my high school had saved a life. He had been driving late at night over a bridge in the middle of winter. The car ahead of him went over the side, fell on the ice, and started to sink. John drove his car to the shore, crawled across the ice, bashed in the front windshield to get the man out (who was in sheer panic mode), dragged him across the front of the car onto the ice, and helped them both crawl to safety. My mother and other women in the Peshtigo Women's Club raised money and awarded him $1000 for his courage. He had never struck me as particularly smart or nice or kind or strong or—any qualities that we often look for. But after I heard the story, I always had tremendous admiration for him.

As an adult, shortly before the following incident happened, I was talking to my friend Lindsay who said, "I think one of the greatest things anyone could ever do would be to save a life. I would like to do that someday." That stuck with me, and I agreed with her.

A Horseback Ride That Went Very Wrong

A few weeks after my mother died, a friend and I decided to go on a horseback ride in Griffith Park in Los Angeles. Maddie (not her real name) and I had ridden together for some years, and were fairly good riders. We were familiar with this particular park and the horses that were at the stable. We decided we would take a long ride, which usually meant two or three hours. I wanted to decompress from my mother's death.

Around 6 p.m., we saw a little path that looked like it connected with another path that we knew. There was a culvert down the middle that was maybe three-to-four-feet wide, but there seemed to be plenty of room on both sides to ride in order to connect with the other trail, which we could see down the small hill.

As we rode about halfway down the trail, Maddie noticed a tree on the right side of the culvert and suggested that we cross over to the left side where there were no obstacles. It was an easy step for a horse to make, but Maddie's horse started to step to the other side, and his back feet slipped into the culvert. Maddie leaned forward and was loosening the reins to ease him up, but he just couldn't make it and within seconds he had fallen on his back, held up by the culvert, with Maddie underneath.

The Accident

I couldn't believe what I was seeing. I thought she must have been crushed by the horse. But when I called out to her, she answered, and I realized that the culvert was holding up the horse just enough that she had not been crushed and was still alive. She and I had made a pact several years before that we would always ride with helmets to make sure our heads were protected. Clearly this previous decision had a great deal to do with protecting her at this potentially dangerous moment.

I tried to think of what to do to help her. My immediate thought was, "I must do something quickly." I thought of several stupid things such as taking off the saddle since the horse was upside down and I could have easily reached the cinch. I stopped that one in its tracks. I couldn't figure out how she could be underneath the horse with the saddle horn and that heavy western saddle. But she was still talking to me. I then said to myself, "Everything I do from now on around this incident has to be absolutely right. I cannot make a mistake."

I tried to pull her out from underneath the horse, but she was stuck. I finally said the most difficult words I've ever had to say to anyone, "Maddie, I have to go get help. I'll be back as fast as I can."

I expected her to plead with me not to leave her, but she said, "I think that's what you have to do." That was a relief, and an incredibly brave thing to say—giving me permission to leave.

When I leapt onto my horse, you would have thought I was John Wayne with the flare and confidence I had. I knew everything depended on me.

I started down the trail and began to pray silently and then realized there was an advantage to praying out loud. I pleaded with God to send somebody to help us out, and just as I got to the end of that trail there was a hiker. She stopped in her tracks when she heard my voice. I told her, "My friend has had a horseback-riding accident up this path. We need help. We need it fast. And we need a lot of it." She told me that her cell phone was in her car that was just down the hill and that she would come back with help.

I got off my horse and left him on the trail. I believed this would be a sign of danger if anyone saw a horse without a rider. It seemed like another potential call for help to let the horse find his way back to the stable. I walked back up the trail and told Maddie that help was on its way and told her about the hiker. I then said, "I'm going to sit a little bit away from the horse, so he doesn't get frightened of me, and I will speak very calmly, but I'm going to start praying." I started to pray that Maddie would be all right and for help to come quickly. And then I prayed, "O Lord, keep the horse calm." At that exact moment the horse started to kick. I looked at this, and I said to God, "That is not what I asked for!" But I did notice that when the horse kicked his body was slightly raised but then as he relaxed, a little bit of the earth from the side of culvert came down, so there was a double threat here. The more the horse moved, the more chance there was for the earth to also move, and I realized that Maddie was not yet safe from the possibility of the horse crushing her.

I continued to softly and calmly pray while trying to keep an eye on what was happening around me. I was very thankful that Maddie was in good physical shape and went to the gym quite often, which meant she had quite good breath support. I was also thankful she was not panicking. We continued to softly talk to each other, and I continued to keep her apprised of everything that was happening around her.

Help Arrives

The hiker came back a few minutes later with a Ranger from the park who seemed to know nothing about horses. In fact, he seemed scared of the horse and probably scared of the situation. He said that the paramedics were on their way. We could hear sirens. Maddie said that the sirens were agitating the horse and for the Ranger to call the paramedics and stop the sirens—which they did very quickly. Meanwhile, Maddie was gently patting the horse from underneath him (I had no idea how she had the aplomb to do that under those circumstances). But it did seem that it was working to keep him calm.

Fairly soon after, the ambulance arrived and parked at the intersection between the path where I had met the hiker and the path leading up to the horse. I knew they were about three minutes away because I had made that journey on the horse. Just that moment, Maddie said to me, "I'm running out of air, and I think I only have about twenty seconds left."

I thought to myself, "No way is my friend going to die when help is three minutes away." I remembered that when the horse kicked, he raised himself up slightly. I also remembered that some of the dirt came loose when he kicked. I made a risky decision that might have cost her life but I think it saved her. I told the Ranger, "We're going to make the horse kick." I then told Maddie the plan: "We're going to make the horse kick a little bit, because he will then raise himself up enough for you to get another air hole." So he kicked and raised himself up a bit and she found the new air hole that was big enough to keep her breathing until these men got her out from under the horse, more than an hour later.

But getting her out was not easy. About four to six men came with this first group, along with the hiker and a very discreet young newsman with his camera.

The men first tried to pull Maddie out as I had tried before, and that didn't work. They tried to call a vet, but there was no vet available nearby. They then discussed how to get Maddie out and how to get the horse's butt up enough to pull her out. They called for more help. They called for ropes. I even stupidly suggested that maybe they had to shoot the horse to save Maddie, but they wisely ignored that comment. On the other hand, I was willing to trade the horse's life for hers. In retrospect I realized deadweight was heavier than liveweight, and there was something about that life force or life spirit that seemed to lighten the load. The horse was helping Maddie.

Soon there were twelve men working, with the hiker and me and the newsman standing by quietly watching. The hiker told me that she had started up that path and right before she heard me, she realized the path she was on was a bit desolate. She was hiking alone, so she started to turn back at exactly the moment she heard my voice. I told her, "You were exactly where I needed you to be."

It still took about another hour to get Maddie free. They finally figured out that they would wrap a rope around the horse's back legs and six men would pull on the rope to raise the horse's legs up and two to three men would be pulling Maddie out from underneath the horse. It still took two tries to get her out—but she got out. She had bruises of every color: pink and blue and purple and yellow and whatever rainbow colors are left. Later at the hospital they discovered she had a broken finger, but there didn't seem to be any other real damage.

The Aftermath

I rode in the ambulance in the front seat with the driver. At the hospital I started to make phone calls. I first tried to call Maddie's husband, but he wasn't answering. Since I was such a wreck and certainly could not sit still, I started to call friends whose phone numbers I had memorized to tell them what was happening. They all knew Maddie and knew that this sounded like quite a dire circumstance. I finally got through to her husband, and he came to see her in the hospital and then drove me back to my car.

When I got home, I was alone because my husband was in Pennsylvania visiting his sister. I could not stop my agitation. I thought of who I knew who was still awake at one in the morning and remembered my friend Kalei from San Diego who always stayed up late doing her art. I called her, and she was a calming influence.

The next day I called a therapist and had an immediate session. For the next three days I visited Maddie in the hospital each day. During that time, she mentioned this was a little bit like combat where one soldier saves another and they come closer together. I didn't feel that way. I felt more distant which may have been caused by the trauma I felt from the incident. I still had not wrapped my mind around it. She asked me to call her mother whom I had met several times and tell her what had happened and that she was alright. I did this and gave her mother all of the details.

I pondered the situation and realized how traumatic it was for me. I needed to talk about it, but Maddie had the opposite response. She didn't want to talk about it which seemed valid to me. She brought up the question of whether there was some spiritual meaning here. Since she was Jewish, I suggested she talk to a rabbi, and since I would occasionally go to a synagogue in the LA area and liked the rabbi, I suggested she talk to Rabbi Judith. It turned out that there was a specific ceremony for those who had survived life-threatening situations. The rabbi and Maddie did the ceremony at the synagogue a week or two later with several of us friends in attendance.

Responses to the Incident

The incident seemed like it was over and was simply a dire close call that turned out fine. But I realized I had a lot of energy around this incident. I decided I needed to do some unpacking because I felt there was far more here than met the eye. The more that I unpacked, the more I felt I was hitting against nuances that were not only difficult, but difficult to resolve emotionally and relationally.

When I called Maddie's mother, she was very thankful that I had been there and that I had been so sensible in this crisis. She, and other friends, felt that I was probably the best of Maddie's friends to be there because I was sensible and stayed calm.

About a day or two later, the doorbell rang, and it was somebody from Nordstrom's with a gift for me. It was a beautiful Swarovski butterfly pin—quite large and very lovely and very special to me. It came from Maddie's mother who lived in San Francisco. When I told Maddie about this gift from her mother, her response surprised me. She said, "The pin was very expensive, and my mother had to traipse all over San Francisco on a warm day trying to figure out what to get you." Deep inside me came the thought, "The mother's response was appropriate to give a gift to someone who had saved her daughter." The gift stands for life and beauty, and it was an incredibly classy gift.

About a week later I heard that Maddie had written a thank-you letter to all the paramedics for saving her life. I felt the need for some recognition and acknowledgement from her. As I pondered why she didn't thank me, it occurred to me that when we know a situation is dire, our job is to keep the other person from knowing how bad it is so they don't panic. Then they decide it wasn't so bad after all. It's obvious to thank the paramedics. Perhaps it was not as obvious to thank a friend.

My desire for acknowledgement was a desire that she know the truth about what had happened. She was under a horse and did not see what I saw. Nor did she know the number of decisions being made to save her.

Definitely the paramedics got her out, and they deserved a beautifully written letter.

I told one of my friends I deserved a medal, and she sent me one in recognition of my courage and good thinking. It was another precious gift.

Why the resentment over a gift from her mother? Why wasn't there either a gift or a thank you or something from her to me? At one point she said, "It was a good thing that you were there to go get help." Later I explained to her through an email that her life was not saved because I went to get help, but that her life was saved at the moment I made that risky decision to get her an air hole. She wrote back with capital letters: HOW DARE YOU MAKE THE HORSE KICK. YOU COULD HAVE KILLED ME. HOW PATHETIC.

I could understand two people having different reactions to an incident that had two different stories to it. And I could understand her wanting to put this behind her and not talk about it further. I saw something deeply spiritual had happened at that moment—especially the moment when I made the risky decision to make the horse kick.

I had several opportunities to write about this event which angered her. I told her I had changed her name and disguised other things about her, even though there are probably only a handful or two of people that know about this incident.

I wrote an article called "Miracle on the Trail" for a small Christian newsletter—with names changed. I appeared on a Christian television show to talk about how I saw God working in those moments and about how I kept calm and tried to make all the right decisions.

My Experience Was Not So Unusual

Several months later, I was on a trip to teach in Rome and had a remarkable dinner with my translator. I told her this story, and Debra told me the story of her saving a life. We began to compare notes on some significant moments in both of our stories. She was with a friend and they had been pulled out to sea by the current while swimming. She had to keep him calm and help him get back to shore as she ascertained he was less experienced as a swimmer than she thought. She realized the situation was dire, and she could see he was beginning to panic and would pull them both under. She remembered a lifesaving course she had taken where she had been told, "You sometimes have to knock the person out in order to save both of you." So she made that risky decision, knocked him out, and managed to get them both to shore. I asked if she stayed in touch with him, and she said they talk about once a year. I asked if he had thanked her, and she said, "He once told me he was glad I was there to help."

Both of us realized we had made risky decisions that could have actually killed the other person or saved them. In both cases the person was saved. I wondered how often saving a life includes these kinds of risks.

Unpacking

I wondered if Maddie's inability to thank me included her concern that her mother was more interested in the rescue rather than the daughter's peril. Was it possible that my momentary closeness with her mother was a threat to Maddie in some way, or did she simply believe there was no danger?

In my opinion, it was far more than simple help that Debra and I had given these two different people. It takes a lot out of you to have somebody's life in your hands. It demands a lot to make all the right decisions with no mistakes. There is no room for error. And perhaps it either demands a great deal of humility from the person saving the other and perhaps a great deal of generosity and gratitude from the person who is saved. I can see that I was not up to the humility task, but I don't think Maddie was up to the generosity and gratitude task either.

The incident continues to have a small hold on me. Forgiveness wipes the slate clean, and gratitude gives resolution. In both cases there is a need for some expression.

It's difficult to resolve without a relationship that acknowledges what has happened.

Linda's Trivia

I have been working with a therapist to understand whether my need for acknowledgement is too much or whether it is a recognition that acknowledgement is simply telling the truth about an event—and that seems important, particularly when saving a life.

Chapter Fifteen
Crisis in Bulgaria

I did a number of team-teaching seminars during the 1990s through 2019. Some of them were with colleagues from Los Angeles or other parts of the United States and some with colleagues abroad. In many cases, colleagues were also close friends.

One close colleague followed the usual trajectory of friendships. We began with a shared interest in the film business. We met for lunches and dinners together. Then we began to turn to each other asking for advice and sharing crisis points, as well as good news and confidential bad news we didn't want getting out to the broader public.

One of these close friends was Jackie (not her real name). Our businesses started at the same time. When she was going through a hard time in her business, I trained her in script consulting, so she would have another source of income. At one of her toughest times trying to build her own business, I gave her $100 as a gift. She told me she wouldn't have been able to eat that week without this money. Gradually we both built our businesses, and she did script consulting and seminars, as well as writing jobs.

Although I didn't know it, she began to see me as an inspiration and a mentor.

The following story appears to be one about betrayal—and to some extent it is—but ultimately it is the story of friendship, mentorship, equality, and integrity, and how ultimately something good and truthful and insightful prevailed.

I had not asked to be a mentor, but I do know that some people see me as one, and I was willing to engage and respond. I was glad to help Jackie—including recommending her for consulting, writing, and teaching jobs.

I'm not sure I was aware of the extent to which I was a mentor for her. This might have been because our friendship was very strong and felt to me as if we were equal.

At one point, Jackie shared with me some of her new ideas about consulting and teaching but felt a bit guilty because she was taking a new path. Because of her admiration for my work, she felt that was a bit of a betrayal. After all, I had trained her, and in her mind she felt she should follow my path. I told her that this was not a Sigmund Freud and Carl Jung relationship where Jung wanted to go in a new direction and Freud was furious. Freud saw this as a betrayal of this relationship between mentor and protégé. I told Jackie that she should be finding her own path and defining it.

Teaching in Bulgaria

In the late 1990s, Jackie called to tell me she had met a woman who put together seminars in Bulgaria. Jackie said she had mentioned me and mentioned the possibility of us team teaching. Although nothing specific was on the table for a job, Jackie told me she wanted me to meet Larissa (not her real name).

While I was teaching in Europe that fall, Larissa was going to be in the same city, so we met for dinner. She asked me if I had time to come to Bulgaria on this trip and teach for a few days. I did have time, but I felt it would be wrong for me to take this solo job because Jackie had made the first contact and had brought up the idea of team-teaching. This was a question of integrity.

Jackie was back in the United States, and I was in Europe, but I did feel that I needed to strongly and diplomatically suggest to Larissa that she bring Jackie over to team-teach with me. That seem the fairest, and I was quite sure that Jackie's work and my work would fit very well together in a three-day seminar. Larissa went for the idea and arranged for Jackie to fly to Europe, so we could do the seminar together.

There was one incident in our planning that should have alerted me to some potential trouble. She asked me to make arrangements to get a copy of the movie *Tootsie* in Bulgarian, but our host said it wasn't available. I didn't get around to telling Jackie until later in the day, and she had a partial melt down that surprised me. I got blamed for not telling her immediately, and she acted as if her entire seminar had to be redone. Certainly, she couldn't have expected the film to be available in Bulgarian, and she knew most participants would not know English. This was another clue that she did not have the experience I thought she had. Snafus are a part of the job and when changing languages and cultures, they are to be expected. I knew that, but Jackie did not.

I made the mistake of taking responsibility by asking the host for something that Jackie needed because in an equal colleagueship, each person should take responsibility for what they need. I had not yet made that policy and should have known better. To me this was a small thing, but to Jackie the lack of this particular movie was a big problem. I had not yet learned to be careful of being embroiled in a teacher's problem. I can be supportive, but this became more complicated than if Jackie had corresponded directly with the host.

I then noticed a new danger area. Jackie asked me to wake her up in the morning because she forgot her alarm clock. As an experienced seminar leader, I had a specific morning ritual and Jackie wanted to be awakened before I planned to get up. I told her I couldn't do it because I had a very particular way I prepared for seminars first thing in the morning. She found someone else in the class to wake her up every morning. I was wondering why she was traveling without an alarm clock.

I had learned through my own experiences to keep as many things under my control as possible and not trust the hotel receptionist and host for everything I needed.

I developed specific rituals over a period of some years that helped keep me centered and calm at speaking engagements. I get up in the morning and meditate, and I usually take my notes down to breakfast and look at them again while eating alone. With a group like this, I simply reviewed them in my room. I slowly get dressed and make sure all of my notes are in order and arrive thirty minutes ahead of my speaking time.

I had also learned not to be swayed by all the things that can go wrong in a seminar. I have given two seminars where all the lights went out from a power outage. I continued to talk in the dark. My seminar in Dubai was interrupted by an earthquake, and we had to evacuate the World Trade Center where I was speaking. In Houston my car was broken into the night before my seminar, and my briefcase with my seminar notes was stolen. Thankfully I had given the seminar fifty times. I went back to my room and wrote my notes. I used to say, "We should be able to teach even when elephants are walking around us and there's a party going on in the room next door."

Although I was better known to the students because many of them knew about my books, Jackie seemed to intrinsically know how important it was for her to be accepted equally by the host. Whereas I wanted to eat some meals with other students who spoke English, Jackie wanted to eat with the host. In European cultures, the guest speakers are expected to do this, but I hadn't learned that yet. I failed to catch this nuance. That meant Jackie was "In like Flynn" with the host in the way I was not. I did not have my political bearing as she did.

I noticed when we arrived in Bulgaria, Jackie talked a great deal about herself and her work to everyone. It occurred to me she was making sure she was equal to me, and I simply accepted that although I found it egocentric.

When we began teaching, I noticed quickly that Jackie's lectures and mine fit together well. Each lecture expanded on an idea. I thought we were both really terrific teachers. We were clear. We were good speakers. We had insights and a good knowledge base. We both did a good job of adjusting to the translator. We would say three sentences, and she would translate three sentences. This went on hour after hour, and we were good at creating a rhythm. We had worked out each day in terms of four ninety-minute sections with fifteen-minute breaks in between and a lunch break. Sometimes one of us would teach for the whole morning or the whole afternoon, but most of the time it went back and forth in ninety-minute segments throughout those three days. We sat in on each other's sections and often referred back to something the other person had said. And we both stuck to our time schedule.

Something Went Terribly Wrong

The first two days everything went beautifully.

By the third day, Larissa had left. I was to speak for the first ninety minutes, then Jackie would present the rest of the morning. Following the lunch break Jackie would speak for ninety minutes, and I would do the last ninety minutes.

Before lunch, Jackie decided to show the movie *Tootsie* in English, which meant that there had to be a translator translating what is said because most of the people in the class did not speak English. So, a two-hour movie—and I knew that movie extremely well—suddenly became a three-to-four-hour movie being shown without commentary, but with translation. I wondered why this decision was made.

At lunch time, I commented to Jackie that she still had another hour and half to go on the movie, and it wouldn't be finished by the time my section started at three o'clock. Jackie yelled at me—in front of about ten students: "You don't care about the good of the seminar—you're only thinking of yourself." I was shocked and speechless, and I think the students who overheard it were also shocked. I moved away and sat with some other people for lunch.

Jackie started to talk after lunch, and it was clear she was not going to stop. She was clearly going to finish the movie and give a commentary. I looked at my watch, and she talked through my 3 p.m. time, and continued to talk through 4 p.m. and 5 p.m. without taking a breath, so I couldn't diplomatically interrupt. Finally, when she took a breath about 5 p.m. I managed to interrupt and mentioned I could show the rest of the movie and then do an abbreviated section on subplots, so we could finish the seminar on time.

After we finished the seminar I told her we should talk about this, and she said, "No, not now." Things were tense.

I was offended, and I felt betrayed. I sensed there were layers of things going on that had something to do with the relationship between me being her mentor and she my protégé. She had put me on a pedestal and for some reason now seemed to need to knock me off. My sense of equality was clearly not her sense. Something was going on that appeared to have to do with Jackie finding her identity, yet I didn't know what to do about this. I'm not sure either of us could have talked much about this at that time or for some time afterward. But I felt there was something profound going on and that this situation was laden with some rather rich stuff, if we could get past the hurt and the wound.

The Aftermath

The next day we drove to the airport with some students. I chatted with the students, but Jackie said very little. Jackie and I flew together to London, and I told her, "We should affirm we did a good seminar." Even so, it was clear deep problems needed to be addressed one way or another.

It was clear we were both upset. On the one hand we wanted to resolve this, and on the other we just wanted to get it behind us. Once we were home, Jackie and I went to a therapist together several times, but we were not getting anywhere, and things were just getting more irritating. I continued having a roiling stomach over this. I couldn't "just let it go." I thought far too much about it. I kept going through it in my mind and felt I was right and she was wrong and that she owed me an apology. However, this kind of repetition got me nowhere. I knew I had to find a way to let it go, and I also knew the right-wrong repetitions were not the way to resolve this. We let our friendship lapse. I wrote Jackie a letter and suggested that we not talk about this publicly because the situation should not be a public display of conflict. People in the film industry like to know who is feuding with whom, and I felt it was important that only close friends knew what happened. We both agreed to this decision. Some people began to suspect something had happened, but we both replied something like, "Yes, something happened, but we don't talk about it, and it's fine." That quieted any discussion.

We both knew that we would run into each other at conferences. I didn't want to go to a conference where I was going to either try to avoid her or have a roiled-up stomach if we were together. I began working individually with a spiritual advisor about the situation. If I knew we were going to be at a conference together, I thought it through and visualized it, so I would remain gracious and I was quite sure Jackie would also.

I think we both had too much integrity and too much respect for one another to only go that far. It was not something we could sit down and talk about because I'm not sure we even knew what had really happened.

An Opportunity Worked It Out

It still seemed that something else had to break through. It seemed important not that we had to get back to best friends, but that something redemptive was reached.

It turned out that we were both going to be at a small screenwriting conference. We were going to be interviewed, one after the other, so I knew we would be sitting in the waiting place together. So, I said a little prayer, "God, whatever you want to do with this to make things all right, I will go along with you."

That's a great little prayer, and it worked beautifully. First of all, the interviewer was late. Ordinarily Jackie and I would have just crossed paths when one of us was going into the interview and the other was going out. But it didn't work that way. We had about twenty minutes or so waiting together so we had a short pleasant talk.

Dinner was the breakthrough event. Jackie and I arrived at the restaurant about the same time. The cocktail hour before dinner was not a standup one, but the whole group was seated at a very large table that held twenty to thirty people. Jackie ended up sitting to my right. We talked about what we were doing in our work and how we were doing as individuals. When it came time to go to dinner, Jackie and I ended up sitting next to each other with her on my right and her husband on my left.

We sat down around 8 p.m. and it was the worst service I have ever experienced in any restaurant. Our food wasn't served until about 11 p.m., so Jackie and I had almost three hours to talk. We never mentioned the incident. We talked about our lives, and we were supportive of each other. We cared about how things were going with each other. All of that time gave us the chance to lower the temperature and recapture the sense of respect and the feeling of friendship between two people who care about each other.

God could not have done it any better. Put two people together where there's no place to go and hope that their better angels come out.

We began to stay in touch, partly through some associations, groups, and conferences. In 2015, I got breast cancer, and I let a number of friends in the industry know about this, including Jackie. Some of my colleagues sent me checks, knowing that there are always extra expenses when one is ill. A letter came from Jackie during this time and I opened it, expecting a letter of support. A check for $500 was enclosed. Jackie reminded me of that $100 I had given her so many years before and how helpful it had been. This reminded me of how much she respected me.

The pleasantness was back. We could have phone conversations and see each other at conferences, and it was clear the matter was behind us. We were no longer best friends, but we were once again good friends.

Jackie happened to be in Colorado at one point, and we had a long talk, not so much about the incident, but about how much I had inspired her and how she respected me. She told me she never wanted to offend or hurt me. She did not remember the incident well, and I felt no need to remind her. We let sleeping dogs lie.

Unpacking

I thought a great deal about this incident. I had a feeling Jackie had been going through a transition. I sensed she had a conflict between her respect for me and wanting to be known for her own work. She wanted to be considered my equal as a teacher, and yet I sensed she wanted praise and support every time she finished a lecture. I began to suspect she was having trouble breaking out of this mentorship relationship. I didn't understand the extent to which she depended on me, admired me, and put me on a pedestal.

She made one comment about this incident during our long talk in Colorado. She said she had to break this relationship for her to be free to have her own identity. She was such an admirer of me that her identity had been wrapped up in me. She also mentioned that one has to force a breakup, almost smashing what is there and do something big to make something change.

Some of what she did was likely done unconsciously. I had a feeling this was profound for her, but she could not access the layers, nor could I for some time. I sensed she felt she had to wound me and attack me in some way for her to accomplish this objective. It was much like the hurt I did to my mother to find my own identity and to get loose from how my identity was aligned with Mom. This time it was done to me. She took advantage of my generosity. In doing so, she marred the relationship. Although the relationship has been mended it has not been totally repaired. We consider ourselves friends but don't share the close friendship we once had. I don't turn to her for advice and wisdom like I once did. Yet, when we talked it was clear she was horrified to think she had hurt or offended me.

Jackie and I have stayed in touch with occasional phone conversations and occasional visits when she is in Colorado. We remain supportive of each other. When she comes to Colorado, I do a private piano recital for her, which has deeply touched her.

In team-teaching, as in friendships, there are layers and nuances, and I sometimes wonder if I have a tendency to not read a situation well and am unaware of the nuances. Maybe. Maybe not.

Linda's Trivia

In Bulgaria, one of my students said that it was very difficult to get a Bible there. I had a small Bible I traveled with and immediately gave it to him. He was so joyful; it was as if I had given him the keys to the kingdom.

Chapter Sixteen
Medical Crises

In April 2008, I was giving a seminar in Baltimore, Maryland. A friend I had not seen for a few decades lived in that area, so after the seminar, I stayed for a few days to meet her and her roommate. It was cherry-blossom time. I offered to take both Barbara and Carol to the Hay Adams Hotel for brunch since I had stayed there when I was twelve while on vacation with my family to Washington, DC. We had a lovely brunch. While driving back to her home, we stopped at a stoplight. Suddenly we were hit from behind. Later we reconstructed that car four had hit car three which hit our car, which was car two, and caused us to hit car one. It was enough of a jolt that we felt it but not enough for us to really be hurt.

I felt sore. I used a heating pad at night. The next day I continued on to see my cousin in

North Carolina, and he arranged for me to see his chiropractor and get a massage. All seemed just fine. The insurance company called and offered me $300 to pay for the massage and the chiropractor and that seemed fine because nothing seemed to be wrong.

In July, I was meditating with my eyes closed and my head involuntarily began to move to the left. I pulled it back to the center and went back to meditating and my head began to move to the left again. Whenever I closed my eyes, that would happen. I asked Peter if he understood what was going on since he was a massage therapist. He didn't know but suggested I go to a colleague of his who specialized in medical and sports massage. She said this was not muscle related but neurologically related and sent me to a chiropractic neurologist in Colorado Springs. He diagnosed it as cervical dystonia, which means it is a movement disorder that affected my neck and, in my case, caused my neck to move to the left.

What Does One Do with a Movement Disorder?

Most of the time, a neurologist recommends Botox which is given with a shot to the neck about every three months for the rest of your life. This sounded horrible. I called my cousin who also had this particular disorder for some years, although her head moved to the right. She was getting Botox shots, so I asked her how painful they were, and she said the better question is, "How long do I sob?" I did not want to take this route.

I went to a chiropractic neurologist in Colorado Springs and did various exercises but did not see a whole lot of change. It seemed that my alternatives were very slim.

The months went on, and it was a time of real deep despair. Every time I closed my eyes my head moved to the left. I simply could not figure out a path to take that had some chance of improving my life. I asked the chiropractic neurologist in Colorado Springs what would happen in the past before modern medicine. She said in the past people who had this condition were sent to mental institutions or committed suicide.

I called a friend of mine who is very wise—Pamela Jaye Smith who is a film mythologist—and she gave me one of the best pieces of advice I've ever received. She said, "Someone in the world is an expert at this. Find that person!"

She also suggested I asked my friend Lynn Rosenberg to do the research because Lynn was a researcher. I told Lynn, "I don't care where I have to go. There must be somebody who can help me."

Lynn searched the world from New Zealand to China to Norway. She found someone in New Jersey who I called, and he said the real expert is in Houston—Dr. Gail Henry. She is a functional chiropractic neurologist. I called Dr. Henry, and she said she had success with treating this disorder. I went to see her for two weeks in March 2009, which started many years of slowly healing.

She specialized in using exercises that pinpointed the place in the brain that was giving the wrong signal to my neck. I started wearing pink glasses to help calm my neurons, and I started doing many different kinds of exercises. I would do eye exercises. I would breathe oxygen several times a day. Sometimes she used electrodes for certain parts of my body. Sometimes she had me walk and sing. For a short time, she had me wear a coat hanger across my eyebrow several minutes at a time and several times a day. Sometimes I would play catch with my left hand or color with my left hand. For some months I wore glasses that had one pink lens and one blue lens. She would give me chiropractic adjustments several times a day.

The goal was to retrain my neurons so my head would stop turning left. Gradually my head did not turn as far, although it didn't yet stay still. But there was definitely improvement each time I went. I usually went to see her every three months or so, and then after some period of time and much improvement, I started going every six weeks until COVID. She was brilliant. She was caring. She was knowledgeable. She was creative. I remember the day that

I could close my eyes and hold my head straight. It had taken about five years to get to that point. I left the clinic, and I bought Dr. Henry a ceramic cupcake as a thank-you gift.

I then had a number of exercises to do at home. Some of the exercises were also strange. With one exercise, Peter would push me in a swivel chair across the living room floor and then turn the swivel chair around to the right and push me back across the floor. Sometimes Peter would swivel the chair a certain number of times, even up to one hundred times in one particular direction. I learned to live my life so people were either straight ahead of me when I talked to them or on my right, to work against the propensity of my neck to turn to the left.

By the time COVID hit and I stopped taking these trips, my head was normal for many hours of the day. Lying down activated it, so I took a sleeping pill every night. Presumably dystonia goes away while you sleep and usually I would wake up and have a fairly relaxed neck. Once I got out of bed, dystonia was back.

In Spite of Everything

Dystonia didn't interfere with my horseback riding and the rhythm of riding a horse was very good for my neck. Eventually, I could hold my head straight while on the horse.

When I sold my fourth horse, I turned to the piano which I had not been able to play for eight years because of dystonia. I discovered my head stayed fairly straight while playing the piano, and I started to commit to piano playing as well as several recitals a year.

When I was in Norway one day I woke up and the dystonia was no longer there. I had done nothing different, but it went away for one day and came back the next. None of the doctors understood what had happened.

My dystonia is not cured but is 95 percent better, and I am now able to live a fairly normal life. I usually use a tone pacer for up to ten hours a day that fits near my ear and conducts a low tone at fifty beats per minute. It seems to keep my neurons in line and is only a small inconvenience.

Dealing with the Mental and Psychological Problems of Dystonia

At the beginning of this malady, despair sat on my shoulder, and I was always close to letting it get the better of me. When I went to Dr. Henry, I began to find hope and little by little learned to compensate and find ways to deal with this. Dr. Henry told me I must fight despair and depression with every cell of my being. She said that medicine for depression is counter indicated so it can't be used with dystonia patients who get depressed. She said, "Do not get frustrated or depressed, whatever you do." I followed her orders and managed in all this time to not get depressed.

I found my theology did not hold up to having an incurable medical problem. It was time to change my theology and recognize that I might be in this state for the rest of my life. Somehow, I had to find a way to come to terms with God about a problem that was improving but not being cured. This was part of my spiritual transformation which I discuss in another chapter.

More About the Battle with Breast Cancer

In 2015, when I was diagnosed with breast cancer, it was not scary for me because a number of my friends had already survived breast cancer. Mine was 2A and had a good chance of remission. The doctor told me the good news that I would not need chemo but would do thirteen rounds of radiation. It was uncomfortable and tiring and most of those rounds were around Christmas time, but I got through it. The doctor wanted to give me a chemo pill as a precaution, so that it would not return, but every pill we tried was debilitating, and I could not continue with any of them. I had about a 7 percent chance of cancer returning without the chemo pill, and I decided it was worth the chance to live a normal life. All seemed to go well for eight years.

I Wasn't Out of the Woods

In 2023, I developed a chronic cough and nausea. I was diagnosed with a variety of medical problems that didn't seem to fit together. I went to a number of doctors and discovered I had a paralyzed left vocal cord. My right vocal cord was compensating well, therefore I was continuing to talk normally. The doctor didn't know why this was happening.

Another doctor diagnosed that I had an elevated and paralyzed left diaphragm. There wasn't much to do about this. The cardiologist told me that my left lung wasn't working. The gastroenterologist told me the nausea was not from acid reflux or other common problems. By this time, I was throwing up almost daily. The neurologist couldn't see anything wrong with my brain that would cause any of these problems. Nerves were checked. I went to the pulmonologist, and he could see there were some nodules but said they weren't unusual. There were other procedures checking other things, but nothing was solving the mystery of what was wrong. I applied to the Mayo Clinic, but they turned me down.

A friend who is a retired MD suggested I go back to my oncologist who immediately saw the problem. She ran a few more tests and diagnosed stage four metastatic cancer. She said it was serious. She suggested a treatment plan that would include a chemo pill that was new on the market which had been fairly successful. Since it was two weeks before I was to give a birthday recital, I asked if we could start the treatment plan after my birthday, and she agreed that should be fine.

I started treatment on August 28, 2023. The treatment plan has been successful. The four tumors were gone within six weeks. I was able to tolerate this chemo pill. A friend suggested I get a palliative care team to deal with the side effects which include back pain, nausea, and fatigue. After eight tries, we found a pill that handled the nausea and after three tries we found a pill to handle the back pain. I started physical pool therapy for the fatigue and have made various life changes to have the best quality of life possible.

I color every morning while listening to music. I take piano lessons and practice piano. For many months I didn't go to many activities. Some days I rested once or twice a day. Slowly I started to improve and do more. I am now able to go out to dinner, attend concerts, go to a play or a movie, and go on short three-day vacations. I recognize resting is going to be a part of my life wherever I am.

Unpacking

I have managed to stay relatively content and keep a good attitude as I have struggled with cancer. I think dystonia was such a tough trial for me that cancer seems a little simpler and less traumatic. I am doing activities that help my quality of life and I make that a top priority. I structure my days with a sense of what I have to do to deal with my health and feel alright about this phase of my life. The doctor believes I will be around for some years because the treatment is working quite well and she has patients who are doing well after eleven years with this regime. I'm starting year two.

Linda's Trivia

I am learning the many stages of contentment, the old and the new normal, and I am continuing to seek happiness but haven't found it yet.

Part Four: Transformations

Chapter Seventeen
Of Boys and Men

I didn't have a brother but wish I did. My family consisted of my older sister Holly, my mom Agnes, and my dad Linus. It was pretty hard to figure out anything about boys. Holly and I knew they were different. They had this extra "thing" between their legs that awakened our curiosity, but it was really difficult to figure out how to see one of those. We think they were called wieners—although that got a little confusing because we had hot dogs at times and sometimes they were called wieners, but then we would giggle. So I decided to call them a hot dog, so I didn't get confused.

Thankfully, Mom had a friend who had five kids, and one of them was a boy my age—Ralph. So, on one visit, we decided that we would all change clothes in our big upstairs bathroom. We had to keep it a secret, and it had to be carefully worked out. Probably our giggles alerted Mom who came up and separated us. It was clear this was not to be done. I can't remember if we got a peek or not, but clearly it wasn't enough to satisfy our curious minds.

We did figure out that if we rolled up toilet paper like you roll up a cigarette and put it somewhere between our little legs, we could come somewhat close to what they had. So, we did that, but that had to be very secret as well.

When Holly and I would draw our little stick figures on a chalkboard, we didn't add anatomical details. But one time Holly added them to a picture—just a little wiener sticking out. I was horrified and terribly pleased at how daring she was. And she quickly erased it. So, when she did it the next time, I quickly called for Mom to come in and see Holly's picture. Holly quickly erased that extra detail before Mom arrived, so there was nothing different about our stick person. I decided to add the little extra detail, and I carefully took the chalk and drew that little line that showed the difference between a girl and a boy. We got spanked for that one. This was the end of my art career in erotica.

But it wasn't the end of my interest with boys. Billy Ewald moved to town when I was about seven and even came to our church which was an extra bonus. Not that my affection from a distance was returned. Then he moved away, although I think by that time I had lost interest.

I fell in love with my cousin Phil whom we saw every summer in Minneapolis, and once in a while their family would come to see us in Peshtigo. From a young age we played in the sandbox together. When we were little bit older, they taught us how to do a snipe hunt. We would go swimming together in the big pool. I began to lose romantic interest when I was around eight or nine.

By eighth grade, I thought that Dale (Rudy) Rudolph was a most interesting boy. He was cute. He had a big grin. He was really good at running and baseball and football and basketball—all those things girls didn't do back then. He wasn't very smart, and there was a wrinkle because he had started to date Susan, who was a really good student and my competition from late grade school through high school. I did hear later that she and Rudy had kissed each other in eighth grade.

If I Only Had a Brother

I kept thinking that if I only had a brother, the mystery of boys would be easier. Then, when I was nine years old, I learned I actually did have a brother named Johnny. Johnny was the oldest child from my dad's first marriage. Dad was about twenty-five years older than Mom, so when I was born, Johnny was in his early twenties. I didn't know about Johnny until I was around eight years old when the neighbor lady mentioned him. I didn't know what she was talking about. I went back and asked Mom, and she was angry that the neighbor lady told us about Johnny. I later found out Johnny had died in the Korean War when I was about five.

I knew from the time I was very young that I had a half-sister from my dad's first marriage—Barbs. She was married to Chuck, who was a used-car salesman in California. Every summer they came out to see us for a week. Chuck would tell us stories every night on the porch—usually science-fiction stories. We knew all of the planets by the time we were six or seven and, in the stories, had traveled to a good number of them.

Chuck was fun and charming and handsome, and he had been on television to sell his used cars. That was quite impressive. For a number of years, their visits were great fun. Chuck and Barbs and the two little kids moved back to Wisconsin when I was in late grade school. Then they got divorced, so I lost my relationship with my brother-in-law.

I still thought it would be cool to have a brother. Girls that had brothers seemed much more comfortable with boys than I did. They got invited to proms. They had boyfriends. They seemed to be able to talk to boys and knew what to do.

When I was fifteen—lo and behold—I found out I did have a brother and he wasn't dead.

He was the third child of dad's from his first marriage. When dad's first wife Harriet left, she took Fred with her. Fred was two years old at the time and had allergies and Dad did not want to move so she took Fred to Arizona and then got a divorce. Later she moved to the San Jose area in California.

Dad and Fred had completely lost touch until Fred decided he wanted to reconnect. It was 1962, the year of the Seattle World Fair, and Fred suggested that we all take the train and come out to Seattle and spend a week with them. They had three little boys—one of them just a baby. Fred was married to Mary, who was elegant and stylish. I liked him.

As the years went on, I kept in touch with Fred. As adults, Fred and I had a good connection. Fred lived near San Francisco when I was going to graduate school at seminary in Berkeley. We saw each other several times and began to develop an adult relationship. Then he moved to Tucson. Barbs and Mom also moved to Tucson after my father died. Mom developed a wonderful relationship with Fred, and when

I would visit, we would always spend time with him. Mom told me at one point that Fred liked to "get people's goat," so Mom made sure he didn't get her goat. I decided he wouldn't get mine either, which made for a good relationship.

Romantic Illusions

Mom was far more visionary than many women of the post-World War II generation. But she also fit into all those stories of 1950s women who wanted a man, fell in love at first sight, got married, and had several adorable children. We learned about love from Doris Day and Debbie Reynolds, whose movies taught us that women need to sing beautifully so a man would automatically fall in love with them. We learned what a woman was supposed to look like from the Marilyn Monroe movies. Although we weren't allowed to go to her movies, we got the message.

We were taught the myths of the 1950s. Of course, we were going to college—but hopefully by the end of college we would have a guy and become a MRS. If it didn't happen, then you went to graduate school and hoped it would happen there.

So, after college, on to graduate school I went with high hopes. I started working on my MA degree in theater at Northwestern University.

Holly lived out the myth of love at first sight. She moved to New York City, met Gunther in early September, and they were married on New Year's Eve.

It was just like Mother thought that things should happen. Gunther was funny and charming, and he thought Holly was gorgeous, which she was. We knew that you weren't to have sex before marriage and that you got married to have sex, and you were expected to be in love as well. So, it added extra stars to my eyes to see them going off on a New Year's Eve honeymoon someplace in New York State.

And it made me depressed as well—but Holly was my role model for falling in love.

And Then I Fell in Love

By February, I had met Albert Kennedy Williams III. From the moment he walked into the room, I was smitten. He played guitar and wrote songs—which is what really cool guys did in the late 1960s. He introduced me to all the folk singers from this period: Peter, Paul, and Mary and Ian and Sylvia and Sonny and Cher. He introduced me to almost-sex, and I had just enough willpower to say *no* and to recognize that after six weeks of being madly in love, this didn't have a whole lot of other places to go. I could understand the song "I Can't Get No Satisfaction," and I couldn't figure out a way around it.

I had no idea what to do with an MA in drama. I had no idea how to get a job. Thankfully I was saved because the guy who was the minister at Holly's wedding had a friend in Vietnam who wanted a pen pal. I started writing to him. I was willing to write to him because I was in favor of the Vietnam war at the time and actually thought they should just go and bomb North Vietnam and Cambodia and be done with it. My attitude did change over the years.

When Mike (not his real name) returned from Vietnam, he asked me if he could send me an airline ticket to meet him in Washington, DC. I was all for the idea because life at school was all work and no play—going to classes, studying, working at the Children's Theater in Evanston five nights a week—and the thought of a little vacation was a big breath of relief.

Mom helped me buy clothes for this trip. My mother had such stars in her eyes about love at first sight that I was suckered in by my culture. Mike wasn't terribly attractive, but we had a good time, and we started flying back and forth between Chicago and DC from April to August 1968. He took me all around to places like Williamsburg, DC, and Northern Virginia. He was smart and a fairly good conversationalist. And he was my way "out" because I couldn't see continuing to go to graduate school to find a guy because that's how my cultural brain was set up. I was almost twenty-three and learned from my grandfather: "If you aren't married by the time you're twenty-three, you might as well forget it." We got married the day before my twenty-third birthday, August 26, 1968. Whew—that was a close one!

Married to Mike

Just like Holly—we met and married in about four months. What was I thinking? Marriage with Mike was miserable. He didn't give me a birthday gift the day after our wedding nor a card nor say *Happy Birthday* to me. We lived in a downstairs garden apartment where all the windows were slightly above our heads. He stole furniture from the Army to furnish our apartment.

He wanted me to make steak almost every night but only gave me enough money to make chicken. He expected gourmet meals and handed me the Julia Child *Volume 2 French Cookbook*, which was my introduction to cooking. I was expected to make his breakfast, lunch, and dinner, and I was to make sure I was home over lunch when he came back to eat. I was expected to pick up his clothes, which he threw on the floor. He was highly critical and once began criticizing my earlobes. That has got to be the bottom of the barrel and was a good metaphor for the whole marriage.

I wasn't allowed to fast forward his tape recorder to listen to music because he didn't think I was capable of such a complex action. I was allowed to turn it on and listen to whatever music he had set up. The music would just sweep over me with its beauty, because there was no beauty in my life.

He was not a good guy. My mother said later, "Look at the core of the person." And when I looked at his core, it wasn't good.

It's true Vietnam was the background of so much going on, but the problem was far deeper than a faraway war because he had not been in combat but had an office job. At the time of our marriage, he was Captain in the Reserves, and he oversaw the Reserve Training. We went back to Peshtigo for Christmas, and he was rude to my mother's friends. He would interrupt our singing when we were having fun. One of the neighbors, Elaine, asked my mom how things were going with Mike and me, and my mother admitted, "Not too good."

Elaine said to Mom, "The light has gone out of Linda. I can see she's very sad."

Nevertheless, Mike and I returned to Sharon, Pennsylvania, where we were living, and Mike decided to leave the Army after that year and go to graduate school to study history. I wasn't sure I was going to make it through the months from now until then. I started to develop stomach problems. I was looking for outlets, and I directed a play for the little theater in town and was a lead in their play, *A Thousand Clowns*. I got the worst review that anyone would ever get—it said, "Linda was also in the play." I was the lead, and they were trying to be nice.

I read a lot. We joined a group that studied racism. I remained miserable. But I couldn't figure out how to get clarity about what to do about this.

How Do I Get Out of This Marriage?

I turned to my friend Mandy and visited her for a week in Arizona, hoping to get clarity about this marriage.

Before I left, I asked Mike not to contact me for that week, although he reminded me that he had a gun in the house and he might blow his brains out if I didn't come back. I didn't fall for the threat. I asked Mother not to contact me either, and she agreed although she did have Holly call and tell me that whatever I decided, the family would support me. A gracious call from Holly was fine with me.

The more Mandy and I talked, the more it became clear that I had to leave. I got on the plane, knowing that I had to go back for several weeks because I was the lead in a play that would have a three-night run. When I arrived home, Mike had filled our little apartment with daffodils and heather—two of my favorite flowers. And that period of time of being in the play gave him enough time to convince me to stay. It also helped me understand I could not leave while Mike was there.

Shortly after that, I got a job in the box office for the John Kendall Players, which was a professional summer theater in Youngstown, Ohio. The drive was only about twenty minutes from where we lived, but every day as I drove to my job, my heart sank deeper. More and more I realized I could never bring a child into this relationship. I was into my fundamentalist stage of religion at that time. And according to the Bible—or at least according to the fundamentalist interpretation of the Bible—divorce was a "no no." You just simply have to love a little harder. It didn't make a lot of sense that a loving God would want me to stay there. It also seemed like the unforgivable sin. I could kill someone and serve time and get out and start my life again, but I couldn't get out of this marriage?

In early summer, Mike had to go to a weeklong Army camp for Reservists. He was about a day into his trip when I realized this was the time for me to leave. I wasn't going to leave without telling him, so when he called that night, I told him my plan. I wondered if he would rush home and go AWOL and make some big change—but I knew that wasn't going to happen. He asked me to call his parents and tell them, and I agreed. I then called my mom and dad to tell them that I was taking the train home. Mom said she would come and get me. She left at six the next morning and drove from northern Wisconsin to Sharon, Pennsylvania. I think she managed to do it in one day.

We spent a day packing up what were clearly my things—a few wedding gifts from my side of the family—and we got in the car. Mom asked me, "Where would you like to go before we go home?"

I answered, "Let's go see Holly in New York on Long Island."

So instead of heading west, we headed east with lots of time to talk in the car. How was I going to put my life together?

I moved to Phoenix, lived with Mandy for a short time, and taught for two years at Grand Canyon College. I then went to graduate school in seminary. My life had started in a new direction.

Thankfully, love didn't end. I fell in love with a cowboy, which was a lovely summer romance. I fell in love at seminary with a Jesuit studying for the Catholic priesthood. I believe I fell in love with him partly because he wasn't available. I'd learned from my mother to judge men on whether they were good marriage material, which doesn't allow one to have good friendships with men or to be able to see them as people and let the romance evolve as it will. Dating a priest cured the attitude that needed to be cured. I could love him for himself and not think much about the future. I also felt this was not a love that would result in marriage, but a love that would teach me how to love for love's sake. Eventually we split up. Later he left the priesthood and got married.

It was almost twenty years between marrying Mike in 1968 and marrying Peter in 1987. My dear Peter deserves a chapter of his own.

Unpacking

In the midst of all of the stars in my eyes, I clearly had no way of putting life into perspective. My dad was not someone I could talk to easily, and I had only met my brother Fred once, and he lived across the country. I had not dated at all in high school and dated very little in college, so I had no resources to draw on. I realized my saving grace had been Mandy. She helped me find my authentic feelings and recognize that this was not a viable way to live my life. My mother also told me I could not take chances with my health and develop an ulcer or other problem over this stress.

Besides my time with Mandy, I think Mother's suggestion to go someplace before going home gave us much time to talk and time for me to come up with another plan for my life. Mom helped me get a job teaching a summer course at the local grade school, while I wrote letters to find out if I could get a college teaching job, perhaps near Mandy. All worked out. In theological terms I would call this "grace."

Linda's Triva

I used to really like guys with a hairy chest until I heard the song from *Kiss Me Kate* which talks about how men might have hair on their chest—but so does Lassie.

Chapter Eighteen
My Dear Peter

I expected to find somebody and get remarried fairly quickly after my divorce. But it didn't happen that way. I was divorced in 1969 and had a number of relationships throughout the years until I married Peter Hazen Le Var April 12, 1987.

Before I met Peter, I dated a man named Pete for six months, lived with him for six months, and then broke up. Living with Pete was like living with Mount Vesuvius; you never knew when he would erupt. Pete was charming and creative and smart—and impossible. I had been looking for charm and fun, and Pete had that. But I had grown up in a very comfortable, quiet household with lots of love and very little conflict. I didn't know how to handle eruptions and tempers and someone who had constant irritations from the smallest things. Pete's fast fuse became very apparent when he and

I visited my sister and her family in New York over Christmas. Pete got dressed to go jogging. He got to the door, but it was raining. He went into a temper tantrum because he was angry at the rain for ruining his jog. My sister started to laugh because she thought he was joking. That only made him more irritated. It was clear this was not a good match.

I suppose I was trying to find somebody who was not like my father who was noncommunicative. Dad was not a negative person at all, however, he came from a generation that was stoic. He was a good provider, but not somebody with whom you could talk about thoughts and feelings. I wanted many of the qualities my father had: He was generous, responsible, a good citizen, sweet, and kind. But I also wanted somebody who was a good communicator. After several dramatic boyfriends, I began to think that what I wanted was somebody who was comfortable like my dad. Mother sometimes said about my dad, "He wears well!"

Meeting Peter

I met Peter at a Quaker Meeting on May 3, 1983. He made no impression on me. The next week I saw him again at the Quaker Meeting and introduced myself, and he told me we had met the week before. I didn't remember. I had locked my keys in my VW, and I was trying to figure out what to do. He said he thought he could get the door unlocked with the use of a coat hanger. It worked.

My friends Cathleen and Susan (not her real name) went out for brunch with me almost every week after Meeting. We invited Peter to go with us, figuring that he might want to learn more about Quakers and because I was so thankful he had gotten my car unlocked.

We had a compatible brunch with good conversation—except when we were interrupted by a woman Peter used to date, who clearly was still angry at him over the breakup many months before. She walked past him and rubbed a tomato on his back. After that we called her "tomato lady." It was embarrassing to Peter, of course. But it gave us a better sense that she was a woman worth leaving.

I think all three of us were wondering if Peter was attracted to any of us. He invited me to breakfast during the week, although it didn't occur to me that he was interested in me. I figured he wanted to know more about Quakers, and I thought it was a nice thing for me to do—agree to have breakfast with him so he could ask further questions and I could fill him in as needed. But we really didn't talk much about Quakers, which should have been a clue. Later he told me it was love at first sight when he saw me across the crowded Quaker Meeting room that Sunday. Somewhere in this easy conversation I began to warm to him. He said something about his family and something about what he didn't want to talk about at this point. I felt a sudden rush of respect. This was usually not the first feeling I had for a man, and many times never thought of how important this character trait was for me. He just suddenly seemed like a really nice and really good man. The more I got to know him, the more I realized this was true about him.

We began to go out on casual dates, including a movie and a picnic. During the picnic, a frisbee was flying toward me, and Peter caught it to protect me. I thought that was very skilled and nice of him. But I wasn't so sure this was a romance. He wasn't making any moves on me, and I had no idea what to make of that. I didn't really know my level of attraction, and I thought that if he kissed me, and I really liked his kisses, that would give me more information. After six weeks I said to him, "Are you ever going to kiss me?"

Peter said, "Would you like me to?"

And I said, "Yes, I think it's time." He kissed me under the tree that was by the front door, and he had "kisses sweeter than wine."

But there was a problem. Peter had these Henry Kissinger tortoiseshell glasses, which were truly nerdy and ugly. I was really having trouble getting past them. One day I said a very superficial and shallow statement to him: "I'm not sure I can fall in love with you with those glasses." I couldn't imagine a guy not getting defensive over that and probably saying something like, "No way am I going to change my glasses. Take me as I am or leave me be."

But Peter didn't say that. Instead, he said, "If I changed my glasses, do you think you could fall in love with me?"

And I replied, "It's worth a try."

We went to the glasses store and picked out some aviator wire-rimmed glasses we both liked. And just like in the Hollywood movies, he put them on, and I fell in love.

There was another problem I didn't know how to handle. Peter had a really weird sense of humor. Some of that might have come from not having the same comfort in social situations that I had. Sometimes he would repeat a word a number of times as if he really liked the sound of it, and I thought that was a little weird. Sometimes he would say unexpected things that might not ordinarily be said in a social situation. Once he asked a bellman how much he was supposed to tip him. Obviously, a bellman wasn't used to those questions. It showed Peter's directness, but it also showed he was not socially adept.

Sometimes he would just be silly and a bit bizarre. He would use different voices. He would sometimes tell jokes that faltered. And I didn't really know what to do with his sense of humor. Thankfully I was in therapy, and my therapist pointed out to me that Peter "got" me. She mentioned that every time he appeared in a dream it was a very positive presence. She suggested I just roll with the funny and bizarre and silly and weird and give it right back to him. It worked.

If he repeated a word, I echoed the chorus. If he said something silly, I played along with him. We began to get each other's rhythms, and I began to experience how comfortable he was.

Getting to Know You

Peter didn't propose right away, even when it was clear we were in love with each other. We moved in together in 1984. But before we moved in, I started to get a little nervous—clearly my divorce from Mike as well as my breakup with Pete were affecting me. I talked to my friend Cathleen about my nervousness, and she said it seemed perfectly normal, and most people she knew had some nervousness before moving in. So, we went forward, and from the day we moved in, I have never had a moment of not feeling really good about this relationship.

Peter and I had both learned a lot from our previous marriages. He had been married to a woman named Lucinda, who had come to Hollywood to write scripts, divorced Peter, and married a man name Sager. This of course was a little strange, and I don't know if it had any profound meaning. He kept in touch with Lucinda for some years, and it was amiable. I admired him for that.

Peter was easy and introverted, which fit me much more than an extroverted life-of-the-party man. I was extroverted enough for the two of us, and I wanted the kind of home where we could settle in. While in seminary I had decided I really didn't want to have children. It was a kind of a lightbulb moment when I realized I wanted to be married and have a career but not have children. By the time we got together, Peter had also decided he didn't want to have children. I was already forty by that time, so neither of us saw that in our future. I sometimes wonder if the artistic and creative output of my life substituted in some way for a similar feeling women had when they yearned for kids.

Our Relationship

Peter learned fairly quickly that I had a song to sing for almost every occasion. I knew hundreds of songs by heart, most from my favorite musicals of the 1950s and 1960s, as well as a number of popular songs. Peter didn't mind that I would break into song, although perhaps that was a little weird like Peter's weirdness with words. I would tell him there was a song for that sentiment, and he had no trouble with me singing it to him.

We had a quiet and calm relationship with great respect and support for each other. We both recognized that we each had individual callings, and neither one of us wanted to get in the way of the other following that calling. I felt that I was called to be a script consultant and author and seminar leader. The seminar part meant that I was sometimes going off for weekend seminars for a few days, or when I started to do seminars abroad, I was often gone from one to seven weeks.

That meant that Peter—once or twice a year—would bid me goodbye as I flew off for several weeks. One time I forgot to tell him I was going to Moscow until about six or eight weeks before, and he just said, "Tell me when so I can put it on my calendar and for how long."

I realized there would be few men who would want to marry a woman who was taking off around the world as much as I was. He never complained and instead went into his bachelor mode when I was gone.

On long trips, I would make out cards for him to open every few days. We would fax each other every few days, and as we moved into the 1990s, there was email (although it was not always easy to get online).

This kind of mutual support meant we didn't tend to have irritations with each other. We had each other's back. We had learned enough in the years before to not be jealous or possessive, to speak out if there was a problem, and to trust each other.

My work meant that I was often going out to dinner in foreign countries with attractive men. I cannot remember any time when a man made a pass at me while on these trips. They knew about Peter and clearly respected that relationship.

I spent my tenth anniversary in Paris without Peter, having dinner with an attractive Frenchman in his home, while his wife was out to dinner with her mother. There was good champagne and good food and conversation and Philippe and I have stayed in touch all of these years. Peter had no trouble with me celebrating—even with an attractive Frenchman.

When my French publisher took me out to dinner in Paris, he stopped the car between the Arc de Triomphe and the Louvre, went to the trunk of his car and took out a bottle of champagne, and two chilled champagne glasses. We had a glass of champagne and he told me he didn't do that for his male clients, but it was a romantic moment without the romance. The French seemed to know how to do this.

One of my most intriguing dinners occurred in Nova Scotia. The wife, who was going to take me out to dinner, got ill and suggested her husband take me. He was from the Northern Territories of Canada and had lived in an isolated place growing up and then went to the university in Toronto. I asked him how that went, and he said, "I had learned to observe wildlife, so it wasn't so much different observing my fellow students."

Another man told me I might have saved his marriage over our dinner conversation. I must have had good advice when he shared with me the problems he was having in a new marriage. He was someone who had gone across the Atlantic Ocean in a sailboat, which made for great conversation.

I treasure these experiences because I had such freedom with Peter. I would tell Peter about these dinners when I returned home. He simply was not the jealous type, and I was not a flirt.

Talking Things Through

Peter and I talk things through. When we were having trouble keeping up the house, I suggested we get somebody to clean for us. Peter was uncomfortable with this because he'd grown up with maids in Brazil and did not like the way they were treated by his father. He had trouble with having an employee "under" him. I asked him if he was willing to do all the housework because my work was very demanding, but it was also too much for him because he had a fairly active massage practice. So, I suggested we see a therapist for him to work this through in order for us to have a clean house. He decided it was okay to hire a cleaning person. We got somebody to help us who was from Central America, and Peter had the opportunity to speak Spanish with her, which was a plus.

One time when I came home from a trip, Peter was a little cool to me. I felt that he didn't understand how one welcomes the wife home from afar. So, I suggested that we have a practice session at home where I would come through the hallway as if I were coming from security at the airport, and then he would practice greeting me with hugs and kisses. Peter agreed to the practice session, and he is now very good at welcoming me home. Usually there is a little glass of sherry waiting for me and perhaps some hors d'oeuvres.

We also added a "non-negotiable" to our marriage. We decided that we would each get one time a year when we could ask the other to do something that was really important to the one person, but the other person didn't really want to do it. If we said it was a non-negotiable, then the other person had to agree to do it. We rarely had to use our non-negotiables because we tried to support each other's wishes. One time I had a conflict because I was the clerk of our Quaker Meeting, and they were going to have a Meeting at the same time that one of Peter's clients was getting married. Peter felt it was very important that he be at the wedding, and he wanted me with him. We both knew it was going to be a difficult marriage—and we were right because they got divorced soon after. I felt responsible to be at that particular Quaker Meeting but Peter used his non-negotiable, and I said, "Yes of course," and the Quakers didn't seem to mind.

When we were in Spain at Christmas, I told Peter I really wanted to go to midnight Mass because we were in Spain, and it was Christmas. I was going to use my non-negotiable, but I had used it some months before and the rule was we only got one a year. I told Peter I really wanted to go, and I was willing to go alone if needed. Peter said, "I wouldn't want you to go alone, so I will go with you because I love you." It turned out to be one of the high points of our trip, and Peter understood everything the priest said because it was all in Spanish. We soon learned we didn't need to use the non-negotiable. We just had to ask if something was important to us.

We had another phrase we could use which was, "I need you to do this for me." That was an automatic *yes*.

Dealing with Medical Problems

Peter had a herniated disc in the mid-1980s and was flat on his back for a number of weeks. I took good care of him, even though I was not the innate caregiver that Peter is. But I was responsible and responsive and made sure Peter was as comfortable as possible, took him to doctor appointments, changed the channel on the television set for him, and made all of the meals. Peter was the perfect patient—not a complainer, in spite of pain, and introspective and introverted, so he could be by himself and had many ways of handling these problems. He realized I was totally there for him.

Around this time, as he was recovering, there was a possible invitation for me to go to Moscow with a delegation of filmmakers. I mentioned this to Peter, but it was clear that he was not well enough yet for me to leave. He said, "I still need you."

And I said, "I will not follow that through. You come first." Several years later I did go, in 1991, and it was a wonderful and safe trip.

Probably my responsiveness to his medical problems finally led to the proposal—or maybe it was just that my friends suggested he practice the M word—"Marriage" and the W word—"Wedding." He took all of this with good humor.

Finally, a Proposal

We had two close proposals before the real one. In the first one, we were awakened about 5 a.m. by the police speaking into a megaphone in our neighborhood. They told us we had to evacuate our condo because there was a chemical spill on the nearby freeway. We got dressed in about twenty seconds. We grabbed wet wash cloths to put over our faces in case we were breathing fumes and headed for the disaster center, which was at the mall. I told Peter that if it looked like we were going to die, maybe we could find a minister among the evacuees and ask him to quickly marry us like they did in the movie *The African Queen*. He seemed willing to consider this. But as it turned out, we were allowed to go back home within a few hours, and the possible proposal was no longer needed at that moment. It seemed to just drift away.

During the barn-raising scene in the movie *Witness*, Peter turned to me and said, "When we get married, can we have a Quaker wedding?" That was the first time that "if" got changed to "when." But that was just an almost proposal.

I told Peter if the reason he wasn't proposing was because he wasn't sure that I would say *yes*, I told him that I was going to say *yes* so he didn't have to worry about that.

Finally, we were on a little beach for the weekend at the Mandalay Beach Resort in Oxnard, California. It was November, and I mentioned something about the spring. Peter replied, "Maybe I'll have proposed to you by then."

I replied, "Oh, I hope I don't have to wait that long!" He quickly proposed, gave me a little rock on the beach, which we still have since he didn't have a ring handy, and I gave him thirty seconds to take it back if needed, but he didn't.

We had a Quaker wedding on April 12, 1987, and rented a yacht for our reception. We cruised around Marina Del Ray for several hours.

Peter the Caregiver

Peter is the dearest man I have ever met. He is sweet and compassionate and loves to care for people. He doesn't do it automatically as if he's a servant and has to be bossed around. He does it because it gives him great pleasure, and he seems to know exactly what to do to make people more comfortable. He cares because he wants to make other people's journey just a little easier. It can be as simple as a mother with several children trying to get the refrigerator door open at the market, and he will respond by opening it for her. Or somebody dropped something and isn't aware of it, and he will make sure to go over and pick it up and give it back to them. On one of our trips, we realized that several people who became friends were all in wheelchairs. Whereas other people might avoid someone with a disability, Peter moves right in with a friendly greeting, or we sit down with that person and have a good talk. He has a natural affinity for responsiveness to people.

Since my cancer diagnosis, Peter has been my caregiver and carries the load. He cooks, cleans the house, and drives me to my appointments, even though I'm capable of driving, but it is somewhat fatiguing. He says he wants to be with me, and he does everything without resentment and with the real pleasure of caring for another. It is always a pleasure for me to be near my dear Peter.

Unpacking

I had an inner conflict over what kind of a man fit best with me. On the one hand I had decided I didn't want someone like my father because of his lack of communication but realized I wanted someone with qualities like my dad had. I simply had to learn to differentiate what I wanted and that I had no need to reject my father to do that. I thought I wanted someone who was smart and funny and extroverted but soon learned that I wanted someone who was comfortable and who would create a calm household. I realized after six months with Pete that I didn't need the drama and tantrums. I simply loved (and love) being with Peter, and he loved (and loves) being with me. I'm glad I figured some of this out and stuck with this relationship when I had no idea where it was going and no idea what to make of it.

Linda's Trivia

Peter and I don't fight. I don't think we have had more than three fights in our thirty-seven-plus years of marriage because we can't figure out what to fight about. We talk it through as needed.

Chapter Nineteen
Spiritual Transformations

The spiritual side of life has always been important to me. I grew up in a small Lutheran church in Peshtigo. We were churchgoers. I measured my physical growth by where my nose was in relation to the top of the pew. We went to church every Sunday and sat in the fourth row, and we sang hymns. I performed every year in the church Christmas pageant. My first dramatic role was at the age of seven when I played the angel who announced: "Do not be afraid" (take a breath); "for behold, I bring you good news of great joy" (I gotta take another deep breath, this is scary) "which will be for all the people" (breath) "for today in the city of David there has been born for you a Savior" (a big gulp of breath), "who is Christ the Lord" (whew! I got through it).

There was the weekly Bible study before church, which I found fascinating, particularly as I got into high school. We would read Bible verses and then we would have a little bit of silent time to make marks next to the verses that affected us. An arrow next to the verse showed it piqued our conscience. An exclamation mark was something we wanted to remember. We put a question mark next to a verse we didn't understand. We then discussed these verses in the Bible study.

My mother played the organ and directed the choir. Holly and I sang duets and sometimes trios with our friend Mary Ann. We tried to live our religion. We were honest. We were what you might call "relatively good people." We had values.

My grandfather was the minister at a conservative Lutheran church in Milwaukee. We occasionally visited for the weekend. We attended a more liberal Lutheran Church in our little town of Peshtigo—although in a small town most churches were moderately conservative.

When I was in high school, I became curious about different denominations. At an early age I discovered that I did not like the highly liturgical service such as can be found in Lutheran churches, the Episcopal Church, and Catholic churches. These churches tended to have responsive readings, a number of prayers, and sometimes the minister or priest sang part of the service, which made it somewhat similar to a Catholic Mass. I found I preferred the simpler services with a few Bible verses and hymns and one or two prayers and a good sermon. My mother had no problem with me going off to another church and exploring and experimenting. My mother said, "If your religion can't stand up to questioning, it's no good anyway, so question all you want." Over many years I have attended Catholic Masses, Bible churches, synagogues, a Baha'i service, and a mosque. And I've meditated with Zen Buddhists. All of these, in one way or another, helped me clarify what was important to me in a spiritual community.

Once I got my driver's license, I would go to our 9 a.m. Lutheran service and then a friend and I would go to different church services that started at 10:30 or 11 a.m. My dad went to a Presbyterian church at 11 a.m., so he could open his drugstore first thing in the morning and then go to church. We occasionally went with him, so I was familiar with that denomination.

When my parents traveled, my sister and I stayed with the Carlsons who were members of the Methodist Church and would go to church with them. I liked the Methodist Church because it had a few minutes of silence during the church service. I liked the simplicity of it. I valued my Lutheran roots, but as time went on, I felt like I had inherited my religion from my parents and that it was time to come to terms with where I stood personally.

In college I decided to explore different denominations again. I wasn't sure I wanted to remain a Lutheran and wasn't even sure if I wanted to remain a Christian.

My College Exploration

When I was twenty-one and in my senior year of college, I decided to do a serious exploration. I began reading about religions of the world. I defined myself as an agnostic and gave myself six months to decide where I fit. I soon realized that I was not connecting with other religions of the world and began to consider expanding my experience with different denominations within Christianity. I saw Protestantism as a continuum with the very liberal Progressive slant of Unitarians, The United Church of Christ, and some Methodists. On the other end were fundamentalists and evangelicals, who took the Bible literally and had a conservative rather than a liberal outlook on life and religion.

Mandy, who became my best friend in college, was a churchgoer. I saw her on the stairs one day and asked if I could go to church with her. She was going to a Bible church, and she was also attending meetings with The Navigators—an evangelical group who proselytized the military and college students. I also attended their meetings and became a fundamentalist. I did all of the things fundamentalists do. I accepted Jesus Christ as my personal Savior on April 11, 1967. I learned the hundred verses that one is supposed to know when you enter into Christianity. I learned to take the Bible literally. I learned to witness and proselytize, which always made me a little nervous and other people very irritated.

I found that I was growing more intolerant. I kept a journal during this time, and when I re-read parts of it, it didn't sound like me. Instead of my religion making me more myself and creating a strong relationship with God, I felt I had simply learned the rhetoric and the ritual, but that didn't seem to be my true path. I had no problem with learning more about the Bible, having a personal relationship with God, and praying—that was a good thing about this. But I did have problems with the push to proselytize and the literal interpretation of the Bible. I followed this fundamentalist agenda for about three years.

When I was teaching at Grand Canyon College in Phoenix, I was getting overwhelmed with literalism and decided to church hop and started exploring once more. This time I was not searching for a religion because I was already committed to Christianity. I was searching for a denomination.

In this period of my search, I talked and asked questions of religious people. I went to some spiritual studies at the Methodist Church. I finally decided to go to a Quaker meeting because it was one of the few denominations I knew little about. I had heard about Quakers when I was thirteen. We were on our way by train to Washington, DC for a vacation. My mother took a little walk around the train and ended up talking to a young woman who was a Quaker. Mom mentioned that Quakers were not Christian, which threatened me at that time until I later learned that some identified as Christians and some did not. I went to the Phoenix Quaker Meeting, sat down in their beautiful silence, and I was home.

I joined my first Quaker Meeting in 1970 and over the years have been a member of different meetings. I enjoyed the peace and the comfort that I got from being able to quiet my mind and sit in silence—although I was and am far from perfect at this practice. I am not naturally contemplative and would not make a very good nun.

Quakerism was good for me because I was an extrovert with a very active mind. It taught me to calm my mind and center myself. It taught me to reflect and ponder before making important decisions. It taught me tolerance because I was intolerant partly because I thought I was right about everything and easily judged others.

Quakerism got me through the tough times and helped keep me calm when things around me were not. My religion served me well and for many years I had reached a level of comfort with my theology to help me feel the Presence that I identify as God and the Holy Spirit.

Testing the Religion

The dystonia I suffered was a test of my theology. I still had the vestiges of fundamentalism that quoted the Bible passages that say if you believe and have faith you will be healed. I believed and had faith but wasn't healed. I wanted God to be my healer and my physician but it wasn't happening like that. I needed to change my theology. I started to think about who God was to me in this difficult time, and every day I would write down a word about how I experienced God. He was my Strength in this time of trouble. God was my Sustainer; He was my Comfort. God gave me courage to continue on and keep a good attitude. God loved me and I experienced that love in spite of the difficulties.

This time in my life was very frustrating. I couldn't sleep without taking a sleeping pill. I couldn't read a book because the strain on my neck of holding the book would cause problems. Dystonia was a daily constant struggle.

I often wondered exactly where God was in all this, but I knew God was there. I was surprised by the elements of my life that seemed to be protected. During this time, I was deep into my horseback riding phase and wondered if I'd have to give it up. The doctor said that riding was actually very good for me because of the rhythm of it. My love of horses and competing in horse shows and taking weekly lessons was preserved.

During the first eight years with dystonia, I was not able to play the piano. Then I was able to back to piano although dystonia had some effect on my right hand. My fingers would pop up and I had to find many ways of compensating by making drastic changes in the fingering. Eventually the joy of piano was preserved, and I could play again.

Clarifying a New Theology

My new theology helped me integrate suffering and a recognition that suffering is a part of life, and we may or may not be healed. What is important is that we love God and love the world God has created. We all suffer at one time or another. Why would I be released from suffering when it was such a part of life? I began to think more about the suffering of Jesus, which helped me accept my own suffering.

There was a period of time that I felt there was this dark shadow over my left shoulder and I particularly felt it when I would take my nightly shower. I kept saying to this shadow, "I'm not yours. You don't get me." I told God, "I don't know who you are at this time but that's okay. I'm on your side. Save me. Be with me." I imagined a circle drawn around me where I was inside that circle with God and with Jesus and that I was safe and protected.

For three months every night I saw that shadowy presence. Every night I said the same thing, "I'm not yours. You don't get me." And one night the shadow disappeared, not to reappear again.

Developing a Sense of Social Justice

My faith is both personal and social. Quakers opened up my mind to other ways of thinking. In 1970 when I joined the Quakers, I began to think through the Vietnam War and what was behind war and violence. I became a pacifist. I learned that did not mean one was passive. I went on protest marches and began to be more socially conscious, first by becoming anti-war and beginning to study nonviolence.

In 1968 when I was married to Mike, we joined the anti-racism group that included members from the Presbyterian Church we attended, as well as members of the Black Presbyterian Church in Sharon, Pennsylvania. When we went to the Black church, we were usually the only white people there which actually was quite fascinating to me.

By the 1970s, I began to think about sexism and about how women were second-class citizens and about all those driving forces that pressured me into getting married before I was twenty-three. I began to experience a calling to drama and later specifically to script consulting. I knew I wanted a career. I wanted to fulfill myself. I wanted to be as strong and as clear and as fulfilled as any man could be, getting the same amount of money and respect as men got. I began to question the whole way of ranking people by who was in and who was out and who was at the top of the ladder and who was at the bottom. My spirituality led me to see the equality of everyone and that women did not need to be submissive or to be in relationships that would abuse and belittle them.

Quakerism helped give me that sense of comfort and peace in spite of the struggle. For a number of years because of dystonia, I could not close my eyes and pray or meditate because my head would move when I closed my eyes, but I still went to Quaker Meeting and stared at the wall and I still tried to be obedient to my spiritual practice in spite of everything. I felt it was valuable, and it was important that I do that.

Peter and I went through a period of time with the Quakers in Colorado Springs when it was clear we had to make a change. During COVID, when we were still members of the Colorado Springs Quaker Meeting, we began to feel tensions with the Meeting. The Meeting wanted to build an addition to the meetinghouse, and I joined the committee. I soon realized the sense of equality and listening skills I had learned from the Quakers were not being practiced in these committee meetings. I had gone to seminary and studied religion and the arts. I had taught religious art, which included church architecture, and I had studied how form follows function, and I had studied sacred places. There was no interest from the committee about anything I had to say. I watched as the committee was planning to build a $250,000 addition and refused to even discuss the size of the kitchen. What was more problematic was the way I was shut up and shut off. This is not what Quakerism meant to me.

I was unsure what to do because I felt very strongly that I needed a personal spiritual community. We started to Zoom during COVID with a number of different Quaker groups, including ones in New Zealand, Dublin, Ireland, and a group in Minnesota and Virginia. We decided to go to the Portland, Oregon, Friends Meeting via Zoom. When we googled their Zoom link, we discovered we were actually in Portland, Maine, rather than Portland, Oregon. Our ability with technology clearly didn't lead us to where we thought we were going. That was just fine. It didn't matter where we went and where we started. We were looking for a community that could fulfill our need to remain as Quakers even though we were not in person. We discovered this group also met each weekday via Zoom for thirty minutes of silent worship, and we started attending that meeting from 8:30 to 9 a.m., our time. We've gotten to know some of the people in the meeting and have taken two trips to Portland, Maine, to meet them and worship in person.

During this time, I realized that I still had a need for an in-person spiritual group. There is a small United Church of Christ four miles away from us in Green Mountain Falls. I had attended that church several times, sometimes when it was snowing and we couldn't get to the Colorado Springs Quaker Meeting, but we could make that four-mile trip. I decided that I would give it a try. I immediately liked the group. I liked their warmth and their welcoming nature, and I found the church service to be Christ-centered without being fundamentalist. I had worked at a United Church of Christ during seminary for four years and was very comfortable with them. After the first church service, I told the minister that I didn't need to search out other churches. She replied, "Isn't it great when you don't have to date first?" I started to attend weekly services, and Peter started going with me. I joined the bell choir and for a short time I was part of the singing choir as well. I am occasionally one of the liturgists during the service—reading the Scripture and reading one or two prayers. I gave the sermon when the minister was on vacation once, and I became friends with people within the community. Within the year I joined the church and am very nourished and nurtured by the community, the hymns, and the sermons. I began to slowly drift away from the Quakers and found the church was nourishing me more, although Peter continued to attend the Quaker Zoom meetings, and I occasionally attend them.

Another Struggle

When I became ill and was diagnosed with cancer in 2023, I quickly found I had made a good choice with this church. People from the church delivered food. Prayers were said. Kind notes were sent to me. People visited when I was ready to sit down for an hour and talk to people. There were hugs. The minister has a background in sociology and hospice care, and I knew she understood the path of illness and had experience with all the stages, including death. I wanted to be in a church where someone would hold my hand when I was sick and dying and keep me comforted and was not afraid of the range of emotions I might have with cancer.

I made several decisions that I considered spiritual during this time. I decided I wanted to be as authentic as possible. I told God I wanted to be able to share my fears and my concerns and my joys and my comfort with Him and with others, regardless of what the feeling was. I didn't want to be in denial. I didn't want to pretend things were alright when they weren't. And, I didn't want to be afraid of the range of emotions I expected to have. I discovered I could do that within this church community and within my group of friends, who tended to have good spiritual values and a strong spiritual faith, whether or not they were part of this church.

I started treatment the day after my seventy-eighth birthday. Within six weeks the four tumors were gone. Within further weeks and months, I began to feel energy, although I knew I was not cancer-free, and the doctor told me I probably would not go into remission. Our goal was to manage the cancer. I asked the doctor if I should plan for next Christmas, and she said, "Yes," and added, "I think you'll be around for a number of Christmases."

For me, spirituality is not a just a matter of belief but of experience. Whereas dystonia led me to make changes in my theology, I have had a different experience with cancer. I had breast cancer in 2015. I did radiation treatments, and it wasn't so bad. I wasn't in pain. The radiation worked. And I was declared free of cancer and even after five years there still was not recurring cancer. This first bout with cancer was not a problem, and I moved through it easily without spiritual struggles.

My Spiritual Response

The second bout with cancer has been different. I wasn't afraid, but I did wonder if I only had a short time to live. Peter was very afraid and anxious as he thought about living life without me.

I was not having doubts with my faith. I felt strangely content. I found I did not want to have theological discussions with God and that I didn't have questions and I was willing to settle into the mystery of my life. I was willing to experience what I experienced and recognize that reality in this life includes pain and suffering and illness.

I found I just wanted to nestle with God. I just let God be in my center, and we nestled together, and I felt embraced. I felt uplifted by the prayers that so many people have prayed for me. I felt cared for and comforted. I felt tremendously blessed having Peter in my life as my caregiver. He is so good at it. I see life as surrounded by the Divine and the Divine permeates all of life. God is the great creator as well as the small voice within us.

Experiencing the Stages

My illness has gone through many stages where I felt lost and like I had lost my bearings. I didn't know what was normal. There were so many things that took so much effort. Even something as simple as making breakfast or lunch, which included walking across the room for a knife, walking across the room to the refrigerator, or walking across the room to open a cabinet, seemed tremendously fatiguing. I found I had to rest every day and plan my resting time around doctor appointments and piano lessons. For most of the year, I was not up to going out to dinner or to a concert or even having cozy long talks with friends. In those first beginning stages, I just wanted to nestle.

It took about a year to be able to start going out and doing normal activities, although I still had to leave time for rest. With all of these changes in the evolution of what I could do, I decided to start working with a therapist to try to understand these stages.

When life was about resting and going to the doctors, my sense of purpose changed. I didn't really have a purpose anymore except to do what was necessary. But the doctors had a purpose for me which was to keep doing those things that gave me a good quality of life. That meant I continued to color every morning, practice piano and give recitals, spend time with friends as I was able, and to start doing things that brought me pleasure while compensating for my fatigue.

This started to change my spiritual life because I didn't know where I was at. I didn't have energy to take on any extra tasks and was dependent on Peter for the cooking and the cleaning and the driving. I was no longer interested in meditating, and the Bible didn't seem to call to me although I occasionally read Psalms. Peter and I prayed every night, and I knew I was uplifted with the prayers of others. I experienced the richness of the hymns at church and was nurtured by my spiritual community there. But my relationship with God was changing. There was a sense God was present but not a strong sense of nourishment from Him. I was simply getting through what I had to get through, and I had a good enough attitude about it that I didn't sink into despair.

But I began to notice moments of grace. I define grace as an event which looks like it's going to go in a bad direction and instead one is given a reprieve and something good happens. It might not happen as we expect it to happen, but there is relief and release. I had been told by a speech therapist that I must not sing anymore because my right vocal cord was carrying all the pressure to speak because my left vocal cord didn't work. I had sung all my life, and I missed it. I mouthed the words to the hymns at church and found them quite profound but knew I must not sing. I prayed that my left vocal cord would come back so I could sing the hymns. The left vocal cord has remained paralyzed, but my new neurologist told me that I should just sing if I wanted because my right vocal cord was performing extremely well. I thought the answer to singing was dependent on two working vocal cords and answered prayer would mean that my left vocal cord was no longer paralyzed. Instead, I got a different answer to my prayer. The neurologist said I could sing. That was grace. My left vocal cord still didn't work, but it didn't matter.

I am just now starting to feel these moments of grace and happiness and contentment and to be open to living in a state of grace. All my doctors tell me I am improving and I work toward finding those little moments of joy and contentment in spite of the uncertainties and the load that anyone with cancer carries.

I don't often do the weekly silent Zoom meetings that had nurtured me for some time. I have found I receive my spiritual nurturing more from the church but don't yet have a daily ritual that I have had for so many years. I am at a disadvantage because I really can't do much reading since it strains my neck, therefore daily spiritual reading is not part of my ritual. I miss it but recognize this is how it is. When I color, I listen to music, and I find my mind is very clear and calm so that is the closest I usually come to meditation. I am going through some new processes that I don't yet understand, and I am all right with letting them unfold.

Unpacking

I have tried to be authentic in my spiritual transformations. I've tried to not be afraid to make changes. I don't want to be controlled by outer voices that try and put me in a box. I feel I have a long way to go toward being a truly spiritual person, but now at the age of seventy-nine I have found a personal spiritual community that embraces me and deepens my faith. I have some inklings of what it would be for me to be a person of more faith where I am more aware of the presence of the Holy Spirit. I am letting that unfold, and I believe my journey of spiritual transformations is not over yet.

Linda's Trivia

Favorite Bible passage: Proverbs 8 where Sofia (wisdom) helps God create the world and she is a delight.

Chapter Twenty
Singing in Carnegie Hall

Yes, I really did sing at Carnegie Hall—with a very, very big choir (160–200 people). On Monday nights, Carnegie Hall has concerts that are not the headliner concerts you might see on a Saturday night but are often good choirs—perhaps extraordinary young musician students. I had been a member of the Sweet Adeline Barbershop Choir for a while, and that choir performed in Carnegie Hall some years before. The choir I joined was made up of singers from a number of different churches around the United States.

Why was I invited? It definitely was not because of my voice. I was invited because I like to say *yes* to new experiences and because I like to create opportunities for unusual invitations to happen.

During my years when I went to Houston to see the dystonia doctor, I sometimes stayed with a former client of mine who lived there. She was a member of the Second Baptist Church—the largest church in Houston. She sang in the choir on Wednesday nights and invited me to come along. It was a good break from being in a clinic for most of the day and, thankfully, Barbara was also an alto and could sing in my ear when needed. I'm a fairly good musician, with quite an ordinary voice. When the choir got an invitation to join several other choirs to sing at Carnegie Hall, Barbara let me know that I would be qualified to join them. There were no tryouts. Obviously, the organizer knew some key people and could trust that the people in these choirs probably knew what they were doing. My ordinary voice probably was not going to make a great deal of difference.

We received our music six weeks before the concert. It was not easy and took a lot of practice on my own. We were given CDs and sheet music to practice with, and thankfully we weren't required to memorize it. We sang music such as "O Sinner Man" and "Simple Gifts."

Our group sang with a small professional group called the Annie Moses Band. Annie was an outstanding violinist, and the other people in the small group were amazing on the guitar and the piano. Some of the program included solos by Annie Moses and other songs we sang with them. We were accompanied by a small orchestra made up of very young talented people, some as young as six years old.

What was exciting for me was going through the process that great performers go through before they perform. We worked on the music ahead of time, so we were prepared. We had a Sunday afternoon rehearsal and a Monday morning rehearsal before the performance.

There was a clear expectation that we had done our work on our own. There was a sense that this is how professionals do it, so when the conductor gets in front of the choir and the orchestra, there is an immediate trust that even the first time through will not be terrible. He raised his baton, and somehow we followed quite well.

We didn't enter Carnegie Hall until the Monday rehearsal. The conductor told us, "As you file into your places on the stage, do not stop in your tracks as you realize you're in Carnegie Hall. Wait until you sit down, and then you can take it all in."

It was magnificent. Red and gold are my new favorite colors! It was a thrill to be in that space and think of all the people who have been there to perform. I had a sense of "What am I doing here?" and feeling entirely out of context. But I felt I was being allowed to get a glimpse of what it was like to be a professional musician. You prepare. You have control over your nerves. You focus on the conductor. You allow the energy from the choir and the audience to buoy you up into a time of great joy.

Saying *Yes* to the Piano

Singing in Carnegie Hall became a metaphor for saying *yes* to opportunities and making opportunities.

This experience began my movement back into piano. I liked singing, but I didn't love it. And I didn't have the voice to perform as a singer except in a large choir.

I had played piano all through growing up in Peshtigo. My last lesson had been during my senior year at Colorado College. I had played duets with a friend in the 1980s but otherwise had done very little with piano for about fifty years.

My fiftieth college reunion was coming up in 2017, and I was on the reunion committee. The committee started talking about the musical *Kismet* that we had done in 1965. We talked about how it would be fun to sing some of those songs. Without realizing what I was doing, I volunteered to accompany the group and that they could meet at our house for the sing-along. I'd had the music from *Kismet* for many years, so I brought it out and started playing. It was pitched at the intermediate level, but since I'd not played much for fifty years, I realized I really needed to start practicing an hour a day. It was April, and I had to be ready in October.

I was surprised how much I was enjoying being back at the piano. And I was enjoying the practice itself—picking up a piece of challenging music and knowing how to practice it and learn it. After five-plus months of practice, we were ready for our sing-along. Our choir director from the musical was in the group and told me I did a good job.

I decided to get a piano teacher and commit to going back to piano. I was already in my seventies, and I had heard so many people much younger than that say they had always wanted to do something, but it was too late. Nothing is too late unless you're at death's door!

I took the leap.

I found my first teacher, Dr. Abe Minzer, through recommendations. He asked me at my first lesson, "Do you want to play Bach, Beethoven, and Brahms?"

And I said, "No, I want to play show music."

Immediately I was pleased with Abe, because he let me lead in the direction I wanted to go, and he followed and helped support me with whatever that direction was. I've often turned to Abe for help with fingering because the dystonia caused fingers in my right hand to pop up. He would change the fingering and sometimes have me take notes with my left hand instead of my right hand.

A few months after I started working with Abe, he told me he was going on vacation for two months. I asked if he could recommend someone I could work with while he was gone. He recommended Sara McDaniel. I began working with her until Abe returned. I liked them both and decided having two piano teachers was just fine.

I began to gravitate to two-piano work and found I had little interest in solos. When I told Abe I loved playing duets and two-piano work, he helped me find my first three duo partners who I played with for several years. Sara also supported this new interest of mine, and I did much of my ensemble piano work with Sara while working out difficulty in fingering with Abe.

We had one piano in our home—Peter's—which was about forty years old. I decided I'd like to get a grand piano. I began my search by making a list of the top-ten piano brands. I figured I would probably get a Yamaha. I went to seven different piano stores—in Colorado Springs and Denver and Houston—and played almost all the pianos on the top of my list—about fifty of them—in these stores. I was waiting to fall in love. I knew I wanted a bright and clear sound as opposed to the more mellow sound that one usually finds in a Steinway. And I knew it could not be more than five-and-a-half-feet long so it would fit in the living room.

At the last piano store I went to, the salesman was ready for me and showed me pianos that were on my list. Then, we came around the corner, and there was a little section of Estonia pianos.

I knew nothing about this brand and had not even heard of it. But I sat down to play it and then stopped and turned to the salesman and said, "What am I hearing? This is beautiful. What is this piano?" I asked the salesman to play for me, and I had the same feeling. I had fallen in love with this piano. I would need to order it, but Estonia was already making a piano of the size I needed, and they would put my name on it. It was a two-tone, which means black ebony and a beautiful African wood. It was a five-feet-six-inch Estonia grand piano, and yes, it was made in Estonia.

I learned some more about this piano. Estonia was a piano company that was more than one hundred years old, and they had made third-rate pianos until a concert pianist bought the company around the year 2000. He started to upgrade everything on the piano, and it's starting to be known as one of the best. In 2019, we traveled to Estonia and had a private tour of the Estonia piano-manufacturing site. We watched the people who had made my piano as they worked on other pianos.

We kept Peter's old piano, so I could do some two-piano work.

Committing to Piano Playing

When I was in high school, we got a second piano in our home. Our first piano was a seven-foot Steinway concert grand. This second piano gave us an opportunity for my mother, sister, and I to play two piano works and do some recitals on two pianos. We performed at several places in Wisconsin.

The world of two pianos was familiar to me. And it probably also followed one of the themes in my life, which was not to compete but to do something very different because I don't like being compared with other people. There wasn't a whole lot of two-piano playing going on in Colorado Springs and none of my teachers had a problem with me going down a different path than solo piano.

Around this time, I added a third piano teacher—Dr. Karen Walwyn. I had heard her play a concert in Colorado Springs, and talked to her afterward at the reception. I told her that I had wrist problems and actually had had a wrist operation shortly after I went back to piano. I also told her

I had some problems with the fingers on my right hand—connected to dystonia. She said that when she teaches, she focuses on the relaxation of the hand and what she calls "healthy piano hands." I decided to hire her, hoping she could help me get around some of the disadvantages I had because of dystonia and because I did not have the same years of experience that everybody else my age playing piano seemed to have.

Karen taught at Howard University in Washington, DC, so we Zoomed and continued to Zoom when she moved to Berklee College of Music in Boston. She began working with me, often measure by measure, looking at what my fingers were doing and teaching me how to place my hands so my fingers wouldn't pop up. She taught me some new ways to move my hands, which got around some of these problems, and what to do with my wrist so I wouldn't hurt it again.

I began to do house concerts and then duo-piano birthday recitals where I invited thirty to sixty friends and rented a recital hall. These birthday recitals were catered and the recital was usually thirty to forty-five minutes long.

One of my fellow pianists told me there was a competition at the Broadmoor Hotel in Colorado Springs for two pianos every January. She also mentioned it was highly competitive—so I decided to go to the competition and see what it was. It was mainly focused on youth from ages six to nineteen, but there was an adult category. No one played in that category that year, so I decided we would be fairly safe to enter the following year. It wasn't as if we'd be competing with fifty great pianists—we might be the only ones in that category. And I could tell that the head of this organization really wanted to have adults. I listened to one hundred youth pianists during that weekend and then began to think about entering the following year.

Sara was supportive of the plan but said that my current duo partner was not the right person for this competition because she was not disciplined. The piece we wanted to play was challenging and would need real discipline to learn. Sara recommended Jan to me, who was a beautiful fit and a lovely pianist.

As I became more committed to playing two-piano pieces, I realized the old second piano in our home had lived its life, and I needed to get a new second piano. This time I chose a Yamaha grand piano—luckily our living room was big enough.

Jan and I played in the competition the following year and won first, since we were the only people in the class. It was slightly nerve-racking playing on the stage of the Broadmoor Hotel, but we got trophies and a medal, and it was great fun.

We decided to do it again, and the second time we also entered a piano quartet, which means two people at each piano and eight hands playing. That year the quartet got first, and the duo won second. We were the only two in the class. That meant more trophies and medals—not that it mattered, but it was still great fun.

Performing taught me how to play with nerves that were working overtime. I learned to let the music carry me, which helped get rid of some of the nervousness. I learned to let my partner carry me, which doesn't take away my responsibility but lets me know I'm not on that stage doing it alone.

That first August birthday recital and the yearly competitions led me to look for other opportunities to perform. I played at student recitals, and I also began to give private recitals for friends from out of town who visited me.

After two years, Jan decided she didn't want to compete again but still wanted to play with me. I formed a partnership with Cindy who loves show music like I do and was interested and comfortable playing in the competition with me. Jan and I continued to play for fun.

Unpacking

Just like with horseback riding, what is important is joy. It is so easy to let nerves get the better of us, and in these competitions it's easy to compare ourselves with the twelve-year-olds who might actually be better than us. What has been essential has been learning that it's important to play the best we can, but our placement and who is better than us really doesn't matter. You don't have to be the best. In the last two years another adult piano duo has entered the competition and gotten first place both times; the quartet and duo have placed second and third, and we were still just as happy as could be.

Linda's Trivia

I feel guilty when I don't practice the piano at least six days a week. But the truth is, I don't practice every day.

Chapter Twenty-One
Trying to Do Better

We're not perfect human beings. We say what we later realize was mean and inappropriate. We do embarrassing things and then feel ashamed. We feel out of our element, don't know how to handle a situation, and handle it badly. Our emotions get the best of us, and we fly off the handle and then realize that we could've been calmer and kinder and it wasn't the big thing we made out of it.

Sometimes we forgive ourselves quickly, and sometimes we hang onto those moments. We just can't get over it because we presume everybody remembers it and that we have hurt somebody and changed their lives in a negative way forever. Sometimes we try to make amends and find out they don't even remember that moment. Other times we apologize and ponder how to do things better. We read a book about the situation and discover that other people have done the same thing and handled it well, and we're determined to be one of those better people.

This determination often leads to a transformation that really takes hold. Years later, we realize that we have changed for the better, and we have figured something out about how to deal with other human beings.

Wanting to Want to Change and Deciding to Do Something About It

Growing up in a small all-white town, I was not exposed to people of other races or other religions. It was easy to be protected as a young child, but as I got into high school, I realized I was very sheltered. I decided to go to a college that would give me more diversity. Even though I was deeply involved in my Lutheranism, I decided not to go to a religious school but a secular school. That was fine with my parents. My mother and I talked about various colleges—I knew I wanted to go to a small college of around 1200 students—and my mother also gave me good advice when making that choice.

She said, "Choose a college that is going to make you a better person." Some colleges seemed a little too hippie for my taste or for my mother's—we were in agreement about that. I chose Colorado College which was in my favorite state and in a city I had visited—Colorado Springs.

There I met Diversity. The President of our class was African-American. There were older students. There were city students, who seemed to have had advantages I had not had in a small town, so I worked at fitting in and figuring out my place in this scheme of things. I remember I was prejudiced against people who were overweight, and thankfully my friends let me know that the person I was talking about was a much-loved student on campus with a beautiful voice, who was contributing a great deal to the college just by being there. I felt ashamed and was glad they set me straight, and I began to work on being less judgmental. I had little interaction with foreign students because I would have no idea what to say to them. I sought out friends that were like me—white and middle-class and nice people that my parents would approve of.

I had few conflicts. I didn't need to learn how to get along with difficult people because I made sure that there were not difficult people in my life. I didn't need to learn to cope, because I made sure that there were not situations that I had to cope with beyond the ordinary small conflicts and insecurities that come from being in a new environment.

As the years went on, life gave me some of the kick that was needed because it's hard to go through life and get along with everybody. I had several experiences that pushed me into changing my attitudes and recognizing immediately that the way I had handled a relationship was not representative of the kind of person I would like to be.

Things I Did Not Handle Well

Shortly after I entered the film industry, I became active in the Women in Film organization. Many of my friends in those years were part of Women in Film and I often began friendships by going out to lunch with people I'd met through that organization. I discovered it takes about three lunches to move from being business associates to a friendship. After a few lunches we would start doing other things together such as a movie or a horseback ride or inviting the friend to dinner, and they would often invite me over to their home. On several occasions I handled situations badly.

In one case I was making friends with a woman named Carmen who was very sweet with an open smile. I thought that she was Hispanic but not exactly sure, and it didn't seem to matter to me. We stopped by her home after lunch one day, and she introduced me to her Black children. I froze. I couldn't put together my concept that she was Hispanic with these children and whether that meant that Carmen was part Hispanic and part African-American or whether she had married a Black man. My near total lack of experience gave me none of the color blindness I needed. When I left, I realized I had totally mishandled this and realized my reaction showed me I was out of my element. My little town might have been a great gift to me in many ways, but there were some real holes that needed to be filled for me to get along in the larger world. Carmen never came to another Women in Film meeting, and I never saw her again.

I began forming a friendship with another woman, whom I will call Rusty. She was attractive, very likable, well put together, and had beautiful reddish-rust hair. We were having our third lunch together, and she was telling me that she had this boyfriend that she really liked, but his parents did not approve of her, and she wasn't at all sure how it was going to go.

I looked at Rusty who seemed so nice and so attractive and asked her what they didn't approve of. She said, "My previous job." I asked her what was wrong with her previous job. I took a bite of my salad as I was waiting for her answer, and she said, "I used to be a Madame of a brothel." I froze and almost choked on my lettuce. I simply did not know what to say. This was way outside my world. She looked at me with this questionable look, clearly waiting to see how I would take this.

Truthfully, I didn't feel judgmental about it as much as simply didn't know what to say, because I knew nothing about that world and couldn't even be authentic enough to tell her that I didn't know what to say or even to ask, "Tell me more about this." We finished our lunch and never saw each other again.

I determined I had to do better than this. I did not want to be a judgmental person. I wanted to be open and accepting to everyone. I'm sure the verse in the Bible about Jesus dining with prostitutes motivated me to find some way to do better and to learn to not only be accepting, but willing to be friends with all kinds of people with all kinds of pasts.

Meeting Candida Royalle

When I was writing my book *When Women Call the Shots* in the mid-1990s, I was doing a series of interviews to inform various chapters in the book. I interviewed women writers and directors and producers and heads of companies. I wanted to write a chapter called "Sex, Love, and Romance" and discuss how women might approach these topics and issues differently than men. My husband suggested a woman that I might want to interview. This woman directed adult entertainment—sometimes called pornography—from a female point of view. Her name was Candida Royalle, and presumably she was quite well known within this arena. I expected she probably had something interesting to say about the subject.

My husband explained to me how he knew about her. I would go off on these trips to Europe to teach—sometimes for a few weeks—and my husband would sometimes watch her movies. I decided I was game for this interview in spite of the fact that my friends were horrified that I would interview someone like this. But I proceeded and made contact, and we had a phone interview that was one of the best I did for this book.

The interview went beautifully. It was insightful and opened my mind to ways women bring humor into sexual relationships and to some of the difficulties of love that I had not necessarily known about.

After the book was published and I'd sent the book to her (as I did with other interview subjects), I discovered that Candida was coming to Los Angeles from New York, where she lived. I decided to have a dinner party for her and the other women I had interviewed for that chapter. There were eight of us, and my husband's job was to pick her up from her hotel and bring her to the party. He was very nervous about this assignment.

I had no idea what to expect. Stereotypes abounded. Would she be really sexy? Would she have on a low-cut blouse? Would she be crass, even though she hadn't been in the interview? I thought it would be an interesting evening and maybe far back in my mind, I was subconsciously remembering my determination to do better.

Neither Peter nor I knew what she looked like because she had been the director of these films, and of course Peter and I had to continue a little more research on our own and discover her films were very funny and not as expected. Sometimes sex was combined with humor. Sometimes the whole story was quite humorous, such as one about the woman whose husband died after a very long illness, and the brother came to comfort her because "a woman has needs."

Candida arrived, and she was a delightful person, easy to be with, and attractive without being a knockout beauty. She was wearing boots that were much like the boots I was wearing and a blouse that was not low-cut. She fit in and added much to the party. I realized that I genuinely liked her, and I loved our conversation which was animated among all of us there.

I told her to let me know next time she was coming to Los Angeles and we could have dinner, which we did along with Peter. We had several dinners in LA by ourselves, and when I was in New York a short time later, we met for dinner.

All of these dinners led to the subject of spirituality. I am not a proselytizer, but she knew that I was spiritual and brought it up every time. We simply discussed it like two friends talking about things we're figuring out and are important to us and some of the difficulties in relationships. We had the kind of conversations that a growing friendship would have.

She was having trouble with one of her relationships, and I discovered she often had trouble with her relationships with men. She gave me a gift of a book that she had written (which I haven't read yet and probably won't read at the age of seventy-nine), titled *How to Talk to a Naked Man*. But I was honored that she wanted to give me her book.

Sometimes Candida would make comments or bring up subjects from her world, and at first, I would get a bit intimidated and either change the subject or not have much to say. I decided I didn't want to do that, so

I learned not to be intimidated when she made comments that clearly were outside my area of knowledge. One time she told me about someone she knew who had started a little business where men who wanted to dress up in women's clothes could come and pay and try on all these women's costumes. Being from Peshtigo, I'm sure we didn't have businesses like that. I stopped for a moment in my usual frozen posture, and then decided I didn't want to do that. I wanted to be more authentic. So I asked Candida what she thought of that. I told her I understand wanting the freedom to explore and define one's identity, but that this really was outside my experience. She said she had thought much about this area of male-female and said, "I'm not sure what I think about this either." As usual we had a good friendly discussion about many subjects, and always something was said about spirituality, and we would discuss it. She knew where I stood. She knew I was a Christian, and she knew that I had a degree in theology, but she also knew that our discussions were conversational and not judgmental, and I think she learned very quickly that I was a safe place to be.

Not too long after that, she let me know she had ovarian cancer. We exchanged emails and as the months went on, it didn't look like this was going to turn out well. I asked her permission to send her a book which was a modern phrasing of the book of Psalms in the Bible and that if she did not like it to pass it on. She agreed and I sent it to her. She wrote that it did not resonate with her because of her religious, judgmental upbringing as a Catholic, and she had given it to someone else. She also said she really felt the care and the love that had come with the book.

I went to Long Island, New York, to visit relatives not too long after that. I wanted to see her since she also lived on Long Island and probably did not have many months to live. I didn't have a car, and it was not a day where I could easily rent a car and travel two hours each way, so we decided we would have a very long phone conversation, which we did for an hour or two. She died not too long after this.

I treasured her, and I treasured this relationship, and I felt I had learned much about removing barriers.

Expanding My Diverse Friendships

I had a very good friend, who was Polynesian, named Kalei whom I adored. I love my colleague who is Chinese-American—Kathie Fong Yoneda. I wanted to help other non-Caucasian teachers get jobs, but I was not as successful with that intention as I was with opening the field to women.

I met an African-American man whom I thought was a wonderful teacher of screenwriting, and I told him I would see if I could help him get some jobs. I was not successful, not because of him but because I was so focused on my intention with women, I did not turn my intention enough to him. I think with more intentionality I could have done that, and it is one of the regrets in my life because the world would have liked him.

Opening Up to Transgender People

I was very intentional about doing better, and I was becoming very conscious about what I call "stopping places." Those were those places where someone was outside of my experience, and I didn't know what to say or do. Instead of treating them as the fully human being they were I froze and turned away—well, at least that was my method of operating, and I didn't like it.

I first met a transgender person in 2016 when I was quite active at the County Democratic Party Convention. A woman named Misty Johnson was at the county convention, and I couldn't wrap my mind around the voice and the clothes and the androgynous look. It confused me that I didn't know whether this person was a male or female, and my brain just couldn't put it together. Well, enough of that. I had met another stopping point for me, and I didn't want to continue with this way of thinking and being.

Misty gave a very good talk at the convention, and instead of doing what I naturally would do, which was to move forward and introduce myself and congratulate her, I instead just stopped and watched her from a distance. At the next Democratic Party get-together, I did go forward. She was standoffish with me, and I don't think it was because of my behavior, but she knew that I had written a book titled *Jesus Rode a Donkey: Why Millions of Christians are Democrats,* and she was totally turned off to religion. I said nothing about religion but that knowledge alone let her know that I was not somebody with whom she wanted to engage. Nevertheless, I did talk to her and say *hello* at various functions, and I voted for her in the primaries. She didn't win, but she had broken a barrier for me personally.

Shortly afterward, I was at another function with a small group of about twenty people. When the guest speaker asked for questions or comments, I heard a male-like voice behind me ask a very smart question. As I remembered, everyone in the room was female. I turned around, and I saw a rather large woman speaking who I soon learned was named Shari. I was a little brighter about knowing what was going on, and I introduced myself to her, as well as to a number of other people and just talked pleasantries. Shari showed up at a number of other functions where I was, and we got to talking. Our conversations each time became richer and deeper.

She told me she was going to San Francisco for her operation, and I said I would pray for her that all would go well. I kept in email touch with her while she was gone. At one point I dropped an email to her and said I knew that today was the day, and she said she was in the waiting room waiting. After she had healed, I invited her to dinner along with five other interesting people. I made the mistake of presuming that she did not have a partner because I had never seen her with someone. She wanted to bring her partner, but we had a table that only held eight and there simply was not room. I apologized profusely. She considered backing out, but I said I would really love to have her there. She came and was a terrific guest. She was so interesting. She had so many insights about women. And again, I truly liked her. She moved away shortly after that, and our paths didn't cross again.

I now have a transgender friend at church whom I like very much. She sometimes reads the liturgy, which I also sometimes do, and is in my book club, and we've also had a few one-on-ones.

Unpacking

In these experiences I realized I was trying to cross a border. I wanted to be open to all human beings and not put up barriers. I needed to be very intentional about it. I began to see that this intentionality sometimes meant that I would meet people and I would "practice" on them, which meant I was objectifying them in order for me to get over the way that I objectified people who I didn't really understand. I was not treating them the same way I treated people who were within my comfort zone. On the other hand, it seemed to me it was better to go through this little phase and learn to cross that barrier. I wondered if I would get better at this and eventually learn how to simply treat everyone as a human being.

Sometimes I did this well. In 1968 when I was married to my first husband, we were attending a white Presbyterian Church, and the church formed a partnership with the black Presbyterian Church in town. Sometimes we went to each other's houses and each other's churches, and I found I was very comfortable.

I taught at the prisons in Southern California—at Chico, which was the medium security prison, in the women's prison, and at the short-term prison for people with drug crimes that were not necessarily violent crimes. I found I had a very natural, easy relationship with all these prisoners.

I had none of these barriers when we'd met the Nehrus when I was seven or with very wealthy people or with very poor people when I'd gotten involved with a charity in the Philippines. It does seem as if some of my natural barriers had to do with different forms of sexuality and different forms of lifestyles. At this point in my life, I am feeling more comfortable with all types of people and feel I have made some progress.

Linda's Trivia

I'd like to think I could meet a Martian and get along well.

Chapter Twenty-Two
Unpacking the Present

Retirement, aging, and the cancer diagnosis have caused my life to take on different rhythms. Many people who retire might actually keep the same rhythms, perhaps substituting volunteer work for the work they did before. Doing projects they wanted to do for some years. Spending more time with their grandchildren, as opposed to spending more time with their colleagues. Going to symphonies and plays instead of business meetings. They keep a similar active lifestyle, although the events of that activity might be different.

When I retired in 2020, at the age of seventy-five, COVID was still going on. There was a natural progression from the inactivity that was going on in the world because of COVID to a reduction of my activity in retirement.

The cancer diagnosis had a much more profound effect on me. I was ill but without a diagnosis from February until August 2023, seeing specialists who were just as perplexed as I was about this illness. Much of my time was filled with doctor appointments, lab tests, scans, and procedures. These appointments continue since my diagnosis.

Along this journey, I began to make some discoveries.

My Life Was Changing

I was more content than I might have expected, considering my very active lifestyle before. One of the side effects of my chemo pill and of cancer was fatigue. So lying down every afternoon didn't seem like such a bad idea. Slowing down was acceptable to me.

But there were empty spaces in my life. There were times I was at loose ends and didn't have the energy to do some other activity yet was out of ideas of what to do with this excess time. I felt like I had lost my bearings, and I didn't know what to add or subtract from my life or what to substitute. The rhythm had become slow and at times repetitious and even monotonous.

After much pondering about these empty spaces, I began to notice I craved rituals and began to put them into my life. Every morning after making my breakfast I would color while listening to music. It became important to start the day with the vibrancy of color and the calmness and clarity and focus that was helped by these art forms.

If there was administrative work to do, I would do it after breakfast. I soon found that my mornings were quite pleasurable.

I had piano lessons several times a week and physical therapy twice a week in a pool. I practiced piano and rested in the afternoon.

For most of the year after I began treatment, I didn't have the energy to do many activities. I began to learn the value of physical rest like a rest in music where there are times of silence. I learned that if I rested before doing an activity, I was gradually able to add other activities, such as going to a concert or play or out to dinner. I could start having occasional lunches with friends. I learned to plan ahead, so there was one ritual of activity on my calendar daily. I had handbell practice at the church one night a week. I joined a book club. Although I was not able to do the reading because of dystonia, Peter would read to me in the evenings. I began to find a balance that helped me deal with the empty spaces and even value that quiet time.

But Is There Purpose?

My life had been filled with purpose and intentionality. There was always something going on in the present and into the future—whether it was the near future, such as the reading and completion of a script, or the farther-out future when I was doing a seminar in a few months. There was the preparation for future events, such as getting tickets and plans for a trip or planning for a film opening the following week. My life had been as much defined by the future as it was by the present.

Since my cancer diagnosis, the present and the future changed. There wasn't a particular purpose in my life anymore—except to finish this book. This didn't mean that my life was without meaning, but it was without striving, and the future remained murky even though the doctors told me I have some years left. I have a new normal—which are my rituals and my appointments and my resting. But I don't have a new sense of purpose, and I wonder how important that is at my age. I have no projects on the back burner. We are no longer traveling, so I have no preparations for the next cruise or plans for another trip to Europe. I have nothing driving me, no one to impress, nothing big to accomplish.

I am wondering if part of this stage of my life is not meant to be about purpose and intentionality, but is about being and not about doing. This might mean listening to friends. Teaching myself to observe the beauty around me. Going to art openings and symphonies. Allowing my senses to be enthralled.

I have asked a few people who are older than me about this. Those who seem to age well seem to live in a state of gratitude. They are thankful for the good waitress and the food they eat and the beauty of the trees and the sunny weather. I'm not there yet, but I do think it's the trick to aging well.

Being thankful seems to be a way of being present. I am in the process of learning this quality by simply being aware of the good things in my life.

Being Present

This reminds me of all those Hollywood love stories I grew up with where there was always the striving to find the right guy or the right girl and then when they got together and their purpose had been accomplished, it was the end of the movie. But that's not what it's like in my real life. My relationship with Peter has no purpose that I am striving for, but simply to live in the aura of love and devotion and care. There is nothing I have to do to deserve this except to respond. There is no place we're heading because we're there.

It is the same with my coloring. I'm not doing a picture for someone. I'm coloring a picture because it gives me pleasure and it's a lovely way to start the day.

This removes the push for the future. I spent most of my life preparing and creating a future that would accomplish my dreams. The future has become less important and is even murky, and I'm still getting used to that. It's a new way of living.

Don't Worry About the Past or the Future

I have been asked if I'm worried about my legacy. I don't worry about that. It's not in my hands but in the hands of the people who read my books and perhaps look at some of my online lectures and find value in them. There is not much I can control about my legacy, and I am fine with that. I don't want the rest of my life to be a push for more marketing and for more striving and for having concerns about what other people think of me.

My spiritual life has changed as I realize my need for God. I try to turn my days over to God and ask for help at night. I have wondered if it is natural later in life to recognize that we are in God's hands and that is enough. I have done so much, but pushing does not feel as if it is a part of this new stage in my life. It seems more important to surrender to the rocky and the smooth road. Surrender is not resignation. It's a willingness to move with the river and to not resist aging or illness or even heartbreak. I'm at the age where friends and relatives will get sick and die, and I will feel their loss. I want to authentically feel what I feel and validate my experiences. I no longer have to say I feel fine when I don't.

There is a new identity that comes when identity is no longer wrapped up with what I do and how I influence and affect the rest of the world. In Judaism, the Sabbath is a day of rest, and that partly means it's the day when you no longer try to change the world. You might do that during the week, but on the Sabbath, you can let that go. You take out the distractions, and it becomes a holy day. Letting go seems to be part of this new stage of life.

I am wondering if part of this later stage is to move into the core of life that is guided by responsiveness. This means responsiveness to others, to nature, and to moments of joy and generosity and gratitude. It is my hope that it can be just as rich as the rest of my life has been. I believe in abundance and new discoveries.

What will my life become as I embrace the riches of this new chapter of my life?

About the Author

This photo was taken during an interview in Spain, and I didn't even know the photographer was taking pictures. I think it's my best picture ever!

LINDA SEGER, Th.D., is a theologian, author, speaker, and artist who has integrated her underlying spiritual, philosophical, and creative approach to personal, professional, and spiritual fulfillment throughout her career and exploration of many diverse forms of art. Linda has published ten books on screenwriting and eight books on spirituality and theology. She has been exploring the integration of spirituality and creativity since college and comes from a long line of theologians, ministers, and missionaries.

She received her BA in English from Colorado College, MA in Theater from Northwestern University, MA in Religion and the Arts from the Pacific School of Religion, MA in Feminist Theology from Immaculate Heart College Center, and ThD in Drama and Theology from The Graduate Theological Union.

Linda is a well-known speaker, script consultant, director, educator, and author who has received multiple awards for her work. Linda received the Lifetime Achievement Award from the Redemptive Film Festival for her thirty-plus years of work as a script consultant. She is a recipient of the Candlelight Award from Regent University for being a "Light to the Entertainment Industry;" the Distinguished Alumni Award from Pacific School of Religion; the Moondance Film Festival Living Legacy Award for her support of Women in the Film Industry; and the Benezet Award from her alma mater, Colorado College, for innovation in her field. Linda is also a recipient of the Illumination Book Awards, which shine a light on exemplary Christian books, as well as awards for Christian Inspirational, Christian Living, Spirituality, and Meditation/Prayer.

Linda has been a Quaker (Society of Friends) since 1970, and is a member of the Church of the Wildwood (UCC). She lives with her magnificent husband Peter Le Var and their wonderful cat Tallinn in the Colorado Rockies.

www.ingramcontent.com/pod-product-compliance
Lightning Source LLC
Chambersburg PA
CBHW030540080526
44585CB00012B/215